ADULT EDUCATION
Myths and Realities

ADULT EDUCATION
Myths and Realities

Rameshwari Pandya
Richa Kapoor

AUTHORSPRESS
Publishers of Scholarly Books

Worldwide Circulation through Authorspress Global Network
First Published 2010
by
Authorspress
E-35/103, Jawahar Park
Laxmi Nagar, Delhi-110 092
e-mail: authorspress@yahoo.com

Adult Education: Myths and Realities
ISBN 978-81-7273-556-2

Printed in India at Tarun Offset, Delhi.

Preface

In the learning society, colleges and universities will have a leading responsibility for providing continuous educational opportunities. Many concepts related to adult education used in the literature since the early 1960s continue to be subject to controversy. These include "formal", "non formal", "informal", "life long learning", "life long education", "continuing education."

The term "adult education" has come into general use within the last half century to identify two different but related phenomena : a field of social activity and an emerging discipline in social science. Although different, these phenomena are interdependent. The discipline finds its subject of study in the field which is, in turn, dependent upon the discipline for its development. It may be mentioned that in India adult education has travelled a long way, at least in programme implementation.

Adult education programme has been running since last thirty years in the Department of Home Science Extension and Communication, Faculty of Home Science, The Maharaja Sayajirao University, Baroda, Gujarat.

It was decided to evaluate the overall opinion regarding the curricular, instructor, physical aspect and the methods and materials used to impart adult education, alongwith the profile of adult learners and overall opinions of the learners in relation to their age, educational level, Personality and Motivational factors, suggestions regarding the improvement of the adult education programme of "Pragati Center." The data was collected with the help of questionnaire. 125 adult learners, 6 community volunteers and 4 teacher supervisor consisted the sample for the study. The findings of study indicated that adult learners gained from the Adult Education programme but certain aspects needed to be strengthened like components of education, self development, health education and creativity aspect of the programme. However, the adult learners had overall high opinion regarding the programme. They found that the instructors were helping, friendly and confident while conducting the classes. They used appropriate methods and materials, which helped them to gain and recall the knowledge more easily. The instructor were advised to use more number of drama and educational games for imparting education. It was found that Women preferred programmes which were entertaining, economically beneficial and of immediate use. If such points are considered, adult education programme will go along way in the path of success. Sincere involvement and deeper interest on the part of teacher supervisors and instructors will also help in the improvement and the success of the programme. Exhibition should be made a permanent feature of the programme. This could be because the environment influences a person. A person will react according to the environment in which he/she is. Hence, through the exhibition learning environment can be created in which adult learners can be encouraged and motivated to learn.

Lastly, it can be concluded that the value and the importance of adult education programme should be realised by one and all. So that they can cope up with the demand of living and working. The facilities like transportation, computer education, library, child care centre facility, if provided, could make the adult education programme more powerful.

Dr. Rameshwari Pandya
Richa Kapoor

Contents

1

Introduction

Formal education is basically an institution activity which is uniform, subject oriented, hierarchically structured leading to certificate. It is also chronologically graded educational system, running from a primary school through the university end including in addition to general academic studies a variety of specialised programme and institutions for full-time technical and professional training. In short, it is oriented towards the needs of those who can afford full time sequential education rather than of those who are deprived. It is inflexible, has fixed points of entry and exists and is designed for a limited time and so, though the trend is democratisation of education, it is not in a position to reach all the sections of the society, and all the categories of men and women. In addition to this, in a poor country like India, when formal education demands heavy investment of time, money and energy, many families cannot or will not afford it for the female members.

This does not however mean that the expansion of formal education does not open doors to social promotion. However, it does mean that the formal system cannot be expected to achieve miracles, nor can it subdue social inequalities, economic backwardness, socio-psychological obstacles, prejudices and various discrepancies in a country like India. If formal educational institutions cannot be an omnipotent solution for all educational and learning needs of a complex society, then introducing a type of education which compliments the present system is necessary. With this goal in mind, the five year plan's educational policy has two major components. Formal and Non-formal Education, working in close correlation.

It means that, all categories of people in all age groups will be in a position to make use of opportunities for non-formal learning, if and when they need and if and when they want. However, in the present situation, since the benefits from formal education have been largely drawn by the privileged sections, non-formal education is being oriented on a priority basis for the underprivileged, which includes women, especially from the weaker sections of the society. Women have been included among the privileged groups for whom special need based programmes are to be provided with main emphasis on the age group of 15-35 years. It was decided that, along with reading, writing and arithmetic, special stress was to be laid on development of economic skills, which would enrich family income; provision was to be made for recreational and cultural activities, and nutrition and health education. Thus, we find out that, non-formal education programmes are not only considered important by all who are concerned with education as such, but they are gaining popularity with our government too. A separate department for non-formal education has been established, to carry out these programmes in the selected districts of all the states of India.

The Directorate of Non-formal Education conceptually views non-formal education as:

> ... work-oriented education organised outside the system of formal education to fill the gap left by the latter in most developing countries in meeting the educational needs of the out-of-school population. It is flexible, life environment, learner oriented, diversified in content and method. It is non-authoritarian, built on learner's participation, mobilising local resources, enriching human and environmental potentials.

Realising the importance of non-formal education programmes, the government is allocating a fair share of its resources in carrying them out. It is therefore very important that people participate in them UNESCO's report on community development programme points out, "Key to success, in any Community development programme lies, in the intelligent participation of women in it. A woman will be benefitted from a well-planned programme is clearly going to be an asset in moving her whole family unit forward on the road of social and economic emancipation."

Many changes are taking place in the scientific, technological, agricultural and political fields for the development of the country. Similar changes come into the existence nearly in every area of life. As transportation and communication have become easier, mobilisation among people has increased, employment pattern has changed, the homes have become fragmented, international relationship has become easier and inter-cultural relations have changed, and so the everyday life of each individual is affected. Girls are coming out of the home, choosing own careers, becoming more independent, taking more education than past days and holding jobs outside the home. Thus the role of woman has changed. One more role of a wage earner is added to the role of a home-maker.

This new dual role of the woman has affected the art of home-making also. Home-making has become complicated. New level of living and the concept of society are developing. The home of the present days, is a different one than that of the past days. Moreover, more and more man made scientific and technological devices have come into the existence. These new scientific and technological inventions are being increasingly used day by day. Traditional ways of home-making are changing. Homes are gradually adapting to the new art of home-making. Education is needed for acquiring the knowledge of the new art of home-making and to help women to play a successful role both as a homemaker and as a wage earner. The women of our country need to be helped to shoulder these responsibilities by giving them necessary education. This education can be given through the programmes of adult education for the women. The need of the education for the women is now recognised and is given the attention by the people and the government of the country.

Nowadays in almost all the states of India, different institutions and organisations have started to run adult education classes for women. In a country like India where a majority of the women are illiterate. As a result, one is faced with the possibility of becoming outdated in one's own field, if one does not continue to learn. The adults should keep abreast of the changes. For this adult education is important as this is remedial education through which mature individuals and mature society can be prepared. Adult education is the acquisition of new ideas, skills, attitudes and understanding by people whose primary occupation in life is other than learning or studentship. In content, therefore, it deals with all problems of man and society, in scope it covers all population, except that part of it which belongs to schools, colleges and vocational institutions and in form it is as variegated as life itself.

Adult education classes are meant not only for the men but for the women also. Education of the women is as essential as that of the men, because at least half of the population consists of women. It is true that when both are educated they can work hard, hand in hand for the progress of the nation. The national adult education programme – a most noteworthy attempt and a massive programme of adult education was intended to: impart literacy assured follow up and continuing education; foster awareness of right and responsibilities as a citizen, of cause of poverty and exploitation and activities of the developmental agencies and obtaining benefit from them; promote skills formation. Some of the basic assumptions of the adult education programme are:

- Illiteracy is a serious impediment to an individual's growth and to the country's socio-economic progress.
- Learning, working and living are inseparable and each acquires a meaning only when correlated with others.
- The literate and the poor can rise to their own liberation through literacy, dialogue and action.

Non-formal education is one of the major educational innovations of the modern times which is not only trying to meet the educational needs of the uneducated who have not been able to acquire formal education, but also to meet the demands of the modern society by equipping the people with upto date knowledge. Non-formal education for adults is important as this is remedial education through which mature individual and mature society can be prepared.

Adult education is one way of continuing education for solving adult problems. With more and more women entering industrial occupation, the task of making changes in the home and school become essential. Technological changes require the adults to adopt to new methods of work and often new vocations. Everyday skills as those involved in child care, food preparation, home management, health maintenance and choosing leisure time activities are constantly being modified. The rapid changes make it important for the homemaker to have means of keeping abreast of these modifications in homemaking skills. Programmes in adult education should be planned so as to reach the maximum number of women who can profit by them. To be effective an adult education programme must arise from the needs and interests of the people as suggested by Sheats: "The programme of adult education must be fitted in content, methods and aims to the adult student as he is, not as the college or the professor thinks he should be."

If the adult students are to remain in the class once enrolled, they must be stimulated and interested. There is nothing to prevent them from dropping a course that does not interest them. Interests of adults are not vocational; some of them do enroll in courses to fit themselves for a better job, but many are motivated by a desire for self improvement and in skills of everyday life.

The difficulty encountered by an adult women when she tries to learn something new is often due to the disuse of powers rather than to a lack of them. The tendency to be settled in habits increases as the person grows older, and makes it difficult for the adult to adjust to new situations. Thordkike, a psychologist states: "The learning ability is not hindered by maturity, although at times it may seem to be, because of forgetting and poor learning habits." Adult education programmes are carried out by the social orgnaisations, corporations, unions, government agencies and educational institution. The labour welfare centres are run by the government for the industrial workers and their families. There are three labour welfare centres, situated in Akota, Fatehpura and Gorwa communities of Baroda. They have been conducting the different programmes for the adults and children such as balwadi, shishuvihar, shishumandi, youth clubs and literacy. Besides these programmes they have also been conducting the sewing classes for the adult women. These classes are open only for those female members whose heads of the family are employed in the industries. The investigator has come to know through the organisers of the Labour Welfare Centres and the survey of the women that a majority of the adult women do not attend the adult education classes. So the investigator felt that there may be some reasons for which the women do not attend the adult education classes. The reasons may be in a number of areas. Due to lack and inconveniency of time the women may not attend the classes. The women may remain absent from the classes due to the inconvenient classroom place such as poor sitting arrangement and narrowness of the place. Poor health of the women such as general weakness and major illnesses may be responsible for keeping the women at home. The differences which they have in their socio-economic status, religion and social belief may keep them to remain absent from the classes. The differences which they have in their educational level, age and personal background may be responsible for their low attendance. The behaviour of the teacher of the adult education classes, with the women and her way of teaching may keep the women absent from the classes. The publicity of the adult education classes may not be done properly. As a result the women may not come to know about the classes. The subject matter taught in the classes may not suit to their needs and interests. Besides these similar things may be taught which they already know so they may not be interested to attend the adult education classes. Interest plays an important role in attending any type of classes.

Education is a life long process. It is essential for each and every individual because it helps in building the character and modifying the behaviour of an individual according to the needs and environment of a society. Education is an instrument of social change and development. It is most important in achieving the rapid development and technological progress. Education should not be restricted to a few years of life, instead it should be a life long education so that it could widen the interests of educated person in variety of ways. The contemporary knowledge explosion changes the volume and content of knowledge so fast that the knowledge acquired during any period of life becomes incomplete and outdated. So in order to have upto date knowledge and needs to continue to learn during the adult years also.

There are millions of people, who have not been able to acquire even the necessary minimum of education during their childhood because of the economic circumstances of their family.

They are therefore, faced to live unfulfilled lives at low level of income, social status and awareness. There must be some provision for them to acquire in later life the knowledge which they could not acquire in youth. Therefore the organisation of further education for adults become more important. Adult education should mean the special type of education for adults above the age of eighteen years, who either did not receive any education in their early life or could not extend their early literacy by taking the advantage of the educational institutions. Adult education is a process through which persons no longer attending school as a regular, full-time basis undertake activities with the conscious intention of bringing about change in information, knowledge, understanding, skills, appreciation and attitude.

The need to continue learning after formal schooling is over is generally recognised by most adult educators. No school system promises to teach the young all that they need to know for successful living throughout life. The place of adult education in this continued learning is of social and educational significance. Most educators today believe that school has the responsibility to provide continuing education to meet the needs of the complex society. Basic to the building of a sound educational programme in any area of teaching is the knowledge of who are to be taught, what are the needs and interests of those who are to be taught and the problems that they face. Such a knowledge has a special formal or informal. Jansen has stressed the importance of adult learning: "In ancient times organised education was for adults; not youths. The democratic revolutions, the industrial revolution; all were founded on the ability of the adult mind to learn and change." The assumption that learning is a life long process is based on a new fact of life: the rapid pace of social change. To keep up with the changes and to face the stream of problems arising from the changes, systematic life long learning has become essential. There may be a decline in learning due to several factors some of which are: lack of interest, shyness and fear of failure and other physiological defects like poor eye sight and hearing. Thorndike also stated:

> .... That maximum learning takes place in the adolescent years (in the twenties) and adults had an advantage in learning which was related to experience and judgement.

Besides the physiological defects effecting adult learning there are some socio-psychological factors influencing adult education which are "…. The adult needs for growth and development, the achievement of social worth and success and the establishment of interpersonal relation." No matter what the age of the adult is there are certain fundamental needs to be fulfilled. The adult women needs something to do that will occupy her time; it may be a job or some leisure time activity. She must have some successful experience, a home and friends and she must feel that she is an integral part of some group. Perhaps one of the greatest contributions adult education can make is helping the adult to fulfil these needs. Typically then, the adult is not studying as children and youths do for some distant future but to improve her skills in home-making and other practices.

"Adult therefore tend to choose the courses they wish to pursue and attend classes at their convenience. Voluntary attendance on the part of the adults makes a great flexibility in their programme. For some adults making of things for themselves and their families or their homes is a great incentive." Women in India constitute 48.4 per cent of the total population. So, whether engaged in gainful employment or working mainly as housewives they are an important constituent of the human resource, so closely linked to national development. Addressing a national seminar on, 'Adult Education of Women in the changing society', the Late Shri Giri said,

> ….in the light of the important role played by women in the modern society,, her education will make available to the country a wealth of capacity that is not wasted for lack of opportunities. As an enlightened member of human society, an educated woman will help the elevate the levels of home and national life and in fortifying the edifice of socio-economic democracy and enriching the national character.

Women's education in India faces a task of immense proportion in the immediate year's ahead. Recognising the fact that, "Education of women is an investment in democracy," determined efforts have been made to universalised elementary education upto the age of 14 years. Educational facilities have been extended and incentives have been provided to encourage women's education in India. Albeit, we have not been able to achieve impressive results. Out of every five women, four are illiterate compared to less than one of every two men. The committee of National Federation of Indian Women observes: "Though women in India have complete equality with men legally, in reality, the equality granted to them will remain 'illusionary' unless the large mass of them are educated."

It is believed that illitoracy is a most serious human aliment and it is a great pity that Indians have entered the twnety-first century with most of its men and women who are illiterate and poor. Adult literacy programme can be an effective mobilising force in bringing about the needed structural changes for which adult education needs a solid footing and a sound theory of learning.

UNESCO defines a literate person as one "Who can read and write a short simple sentence with understanding on his everyday life." A person is functionally literate when he can engage in all those activities in which literacy is required for effective functioning of his group and community the classical notion of literacy which wide spread in our country is the learning of 3R's, i.e., reading, writing and arithmetic.

The National Literacy Mission termed literacy as functional literacy which implies achieving self-reliance and in becoming aware of cause of their deprivation and moving towards amelioration of their condition through organisation and participation in the process of developments acquiring skills to improve economic status and general integration, conservation of environments and women equality. Development which is understood generally as combination and inter-play of several socio-economic factors and their outcome for general good.

Developments may be equated with economic, social and cultural upliftment in life. It is rated and equated with growth rate Gross national Product (GNP) and per capital income and also related with utilisation of modern scientific discoveries and technology.

In the matter of adult education development adult education means all that has been with socio-economic status having high standard of living, etc., because human factor is supreme in any development processes any activity to educate adults is regarded as an investment for development of human resources.

Along with the Rs which are considered essential for any literacy programmes concept of functional literacy introduced by UNESCO long back and promoted by the adult education and the decision makers of our country since 1970 has not been able to take roots in the field. To improve the literacy level and to make people learn the daily requirements. Universities and other resources centers have prepared good models of the functional literacy. However, we are neither able to impart knowledge relating to the functional areas of the learners nor are able to create awareness which may lead them to improve the functionality of their day to day life.

Many educators and organisation view literacy very narrowly; as they assume literacy should be defined only within a certain context of functioning, which may change from one country/ culture to another, or overtime. Some definition also include as part of literacy—other mental skills, such as numeracy and problem solving continuously strive to understand these various factors, definition—and incorporate this understanding to solve the problem of illiteracy. In our country, The number of out of school children estimated million. The literacy situation is dismal at the global level yet to literacy rate in these region has hardly reached about 60 per cent. high literacy rate of about 80 per cent will need to have a target of improving it by 20 per cent as they can go beyond 100 per cent literacy, but countries with a lower literacy rate of about 60 per cent are required to raise it by, 30 per cent (50% of 60%) to achieve 50 per cent achievement to achieve 50 per cent increase in female literacy rates. All aspects of the quality of education and ensuring excellence, especially in literacy, numeracy and essential life skills. National Family Health Survey- 2 (*Reservoir* November 1989 to March 1999) indicated the adult literacy rate of 58.46 for all persons with a literacy rate of 44.5 per cent for female population. It has been estimated that the number of adult literates would have increased by 157 million in 2001. The number of adult illiterates is estimated to have gone down from 271 million in 1991 to 263 million in 2001. UNESCO estimates have indicated that the number of adult illiterates in India in 2002 was 287 million and the estimated number of adult illiterates for the world as a whole was 862 million, thereby implying that one-third (33.3%) of all the adult literate of the world resides in India. Even taking into account our own estimates, the share of India of adult illiteracy comes to about 30.5 per cent.

For India UNESCO have estimated a figure of 268 million illiterates for the year 2015, i.e., one million higher than the year 2002 figure, thereby indicating that India's share will go up to 36 per cent. UNESCO estimates indicate that on the basis of the existing trends the problem of illiteracy will continue for a long time, particularly in case of low literacy and high population countries of the world.

There is need to upgrade the efforts so that the level of achievement is raised during the International Literacy Decade. For rising the level of achievement additional efforts will need to be made. Strong national and international commitment will need to be created. It will be necessary to take action on the feedback received from countries. There is a need to ensure that the financial resources should not be a constraint in raising the level of achievement particularly in case of low literacy countries.

Ensuring the commitment of international support of these countries is very essential. Special consideration will need to be given to high population countries and the least developed countries. In order to accelerate progress, participation of civil society, NGOs in the formulation, implementation and monitoring of the adult literacy programme at different level is very important. Gender disparity in literacy rates continues to be high in most of the developing countries. Factors that are responsible for low literacy among females will need to be given proper attention. The problem of illiteracy is no more to be treated as a lack of the skill of reading, writing and numeracy. It is now related to the use of these skills and other life skills for the development and well being of the individual in the community, the nation and the world. So it is to be treated as a major part of the social and economic development. The quantitative aspects is much more important factor but the qualitative aspect is important and has to be given due attention by the nations of the world.

India is facing the problem of illiteracy both in quantities and qualitative terms. Serious efforts are now being made through the National Literacy Mission and the Sarva Siksa Abhiyan to tackle this problem. The National Literacy Mission launched (NLM) the Total Literacy Campaign in different parts of the country and has covered 569 of the 600 district in the country. These efforts moved from providing basic literacy skills under Total Literacy Campaign to retention and use of these skills under Post-Literacy Programme. NLM efforts have been upgraded to qualitative aspects of the literacy through the Combining Education Programme which aims at providing vocational and life skills to the people for their social and economic development. The need is to put this strategy on a stronger footing. Deficiencies in implementation and resources supports need to be plugged. For example, Jan Shikshan Santhan has been set up to promote vocation and occupational development of the literates, neo-literates, semi-literates and non-literates. There is an urgent need to set up such institutions in the entire district of the country.

The National Institution of Open Schooling has launched the Open Basic Education (OBE) programme as an alternative educational programme both for children and for adults. The OBE programme has three levels: preparatory, primary and elementary, which are equivalent to standards III, V and VIII. This programme provides an opportunity for the semi-literates and neo-literates to continue their education which can be used in their day-to-day life situations.

Literacy in India is an indispensable means for effective social and economic participation, contributing to human development and poverty reduction, says UNESCO. The right to education is also a fundamental human right. UNESCO aims at education for all by 2015. India is one of the countries (along with the Arab states and sub-Saharan Africa) where the literacy levels are still below the threshold level of 75 per cent but gigantic efforts are on to achieve that level. More than three-fourths of the country's male population and above half of the female population is literate.

Table 1 below shows the adult and youth literacy rates for India and some of the neighbouring countries in 2002 by UNESCO.

Table 1

Country	*Adult Literacy Rate (%)*	*Youth Literacy Rate (%)*
China	91.00 (2000-2005)	98.90 (2004)
India	66.00 (2000-2007)	82.00 (2000-2007)
Nepal	44.0	62.7
Pakistan	41.5	53.9
Sri Lanka	92.0	98.0
Bangaladesh	41.1	49.7

{Adult literacy rate is for the age group 15 years and above. Youth literacy rate is for the age group 15-24 years (i.e., youth represents a subset of adults). The youth literacy rate for India relates to 2001.}

Literacy as defined by UNESCO

1. A literate person is one who can with understanding both read and write a short simple statement relevant to his everyday life.
2. Literacy is not the simple reading of a word or a set of associated symbols and sounds, but an act of critical understanding of men's situation in the world.
3. Literacy is not an end in itself but a means of personal liberation and development and extending individuals educational efforts involving overall inter-disciplinary responses to concrete problems.
4. A literate person is one who has acquired all the essential knowledge and skills which enable him to engage in all those activities in which literacy is required for effective functioning in his group and community and whose attaining in reading, writing and numeracy make it possible to use these skills towards his own and his community's development.

Another way to look at literacy is in that "it is used to create identity" (Dudfield, 1999). It is a state of being able to communicate via text in all its manifestations, and as such, literacy is the foundation of much of our primary school education. The Internet is quickly becoming the most prominent form of textual interaction in the world, and using it demands a new set of skills. Literacy must be viewed in context of its immense potential in the progression towards a virtual transformation in the quality of human life. Its impact on bringing about a paradigm shift in the direction of society progresses can never be overestimated—be it economic, political or social.

Brief History of Adult Education

After the formation of the popular ministries in 1947, some of the states undertook adult education programme in various parts of the country. However, a beginning was made and the movement was endowed with respectability and supported from various quarters. The Indian Adult Education Association, at its conference in Rewa in December 1947 recognised that education of the masses should be given the highest priority. The concepts of social education emerged in this period. The Central Advisory Board of Education at its meeting in January 1948 expressed the view that the organisation of the adult education in India has become necessary. During the period 1949-52 the adult education aim was to enable the members of their communities to work for achieving their social, economic and political development.

After 1952, the adult education programme became an integral part of the planned programmes. Social education organisers training centres were set up in various parts of the country, and public library movement was given a momentum. Use of radio as medium of education began to be recognised and the Ministry of Information produced a number of educational documentaries.

At the national level, in 1956 an important step in the field of adult education was the establishment of the National Fundamental Education Centre, whose functions include training and orientation of key personnel, experimentation in preparation of materials, conducting research and evaluation in the field of adult education.

Another milestone in the field of adult education has been the launching in 1967-68 of a three-dimensional integrated programme of farmer's training and functional literacy. This was the first time that the three central ministries, namely, Agriculture, Information Broadcasting and Education co-ordinated including functional literacy to the farmers in the high yielding variety programme areas.

Yet, another effort in the field of adult education has been the launching of non-formal education programme during 1975-76 in the country and out-of school youth and adults. A significant step in the field of adult education in the country has been the launching of National Adult Education Programme all over the country on October 2, 1978 with the uphill task of covering ten crore illiterates in the age group of 15 to 35. Also in 1978 the universities were involved in a substantial way in the national adult education programme of Government of India.

In 1983, the UGC converted the centre for adult education into full-fledged university departments for adult and continuing education. To implement the recommendations of the review committee on role of university towards the community, the UGC, in 1989, instructed that all extension programme must be conducted in area or community adopted by a university department or an affiliated college. This helped ensure development of a relationship between university college and the community. Colleges were provided with grants to open a community education centre in the community. This centre was to function as the extension centre of the college. In 1992, the university extension departments were asked to ensure that the communities which were adopted by the colleges for eradication of illiteracy and conducting continuing and adult education courses on a regular basis.

Today, universities in the country are involved in nation-wide extension programme through departments/centres set up and funded by UGC. These institutions are involved in programmes like literacy, post literacy, continuing education, and science for people, environmental education, legal literacy and technology transfer through involving students and teachers.

Eradication of illiteracy has been one of the major national concerns of the Government of India since independence. The need for a literate population and universal education for all children in the age group 6-14 was recognised as a crucial input for nation building and was given due consideration in the Constitution as well as in the successive five-year plans. A number of significant programmes have been taken up since independence to eradicate illiteracy among adults. Some of the important programmes are discussed below.

Social education

The main elements were literacy, extension, general education, leadership training and social consciousness. The programme was implemented in the first five-year plan (1951-56).

Gram Shikshan Mohim

Movement for literacy in the rural areas was started in 1959 in Satara district of Maharashtra, and was later extended to other parts of the state. The programme aimed at imparting basic literacy skills within a period of about four months. The programme, however, suffered from a lack of systematic follow-up which resulted in relapse to illiteracy.

Farmers' Functional Literacy Project

Verdan started in 1967-68 as an inter-ministerial project for farmers' training and functional literacy, the project aimed at popularisation of high-yielding varieties of seeds through the process of adult education. The programme was confined to 144 districts of the country where nearly 8,640 classes were organised for about 2.6 lakh adults.

Non-formal Education

In the beginning of the fifth plan, a programme of non-formal education for 15-25 age-group was launched. Although the scope, content and objective of the non-formal project was clearly spelt out, its understanding in the field was very limited and the programmes actually organised indistinguishable from the conventional literacy programmes.

Polyvalent Adult Education Centres Workers' Social Education

Institutes and Polyvalent Adult Education Centres were reviewed by a group in 1977, which recommended adoption of Polyvalent Adult Education Centres in the adult education programmes for workers in urban areas. In pursuance of this decision, Shramik Vidyapeeths were set up in the states.

Education Commission (1964-66)

The appointment of Education Commission (1964-66) was a significant event in the history of education in India. Among several measures, it recommended that high priority be accorded to ending illiteracy. It urged that adult education be promoted both through "selective" as well "mass approach" and stressed on the active involvement of teachers and students and the wider use of the media for the literacy programmes. The Education Commission also stated that in the world of science and technology, the main objective should be to relate it to life, needs and aspirations of the people so as to make it an instrument of socio-economic and political change.

Functional Literacy for Adult Women (FLAW)

The scheme of Functional - Literacy for Adult Women (FLAW) was started in 1975-76 in the experimental ICDS project areas. It was gradually expanded along withy the expansion of ICDS. By 1981-82, 300 ICDS projects were approved where these FLAW centres also functioned. However, it was decided to stop the expansion of FLAW scheme in ICDS project areas mainly due to a constraint of resources. The aim of FLAW scheme was to enable illiterate adult women to acquire functional skills along with literacy, to promote better awareness of health, hygiene, child-care practices and to bring about attitudinal changes. The target age group was 15-35 age group.

National Adult Education Programme (NAEP)

The first nation-wide attempt at eradication of illiteracy was made through the National Adult Education Programme launched on October 2, 1978. It was a massive programme which aimed at educating 100 million non-literate adults in the age group of 15-35 years within a timeframe of five years. The objectives of the National Adult Education Programme were not merely to impart literacy in the conventional sense, but also to provide learners with functional awareness, which were conceived as three integral components of the skills of reading, writing and arithmetic. Functionality implied the ability to utilise and apply the skills acquired with a view to promote efficiency of the neo-literate. The social awareness component aimed at knowing, understanding and taking action on issues which affect the individual, community and society.

Rural Functional Literacy Project (RFLP)

This was the flagship programme of NAEP and was started as a centrally sponsored scheme in 1978 for rural areas. The erstwhile 144 Farmers' Functional Literacy Projects and 60 Non-formal Education Projects were merged into it. Further, projects were added and the number of projects throughout the country in 1987 was 513, each having up to a maximum number of 300 adult education centres and each centre having 25-30 learners, achieving self-reliance in literacy and numeracy:

- Becoming aware of the causes of present condition through organisation and participation in the process of development;
- Acquiring skills to improve economic status and general wellbeing;
- Imbibing the value of national integration, conservation of the environment, women's equality, observance of small family norms, etc.
- The programme of action (POA) for implementation of National Policy on Education (1986) states that RFLPs will be strengthened by;
- Introduction of flexibility in the project structure;
- Greater use of spoken language of the tribal learners (including language spoken by tribal people);
- Emphasis on training of Functionaries;
- Decentralisation of the supervisory system;
- Increase in the number of women instructors, even by adjusting the minimum qualification and making arrangements for their continuing education;
- Continuity regarding duration of the projects;
- Application of science and technology for improvement in environment of the learning centers, greater use of education technology and research in pedagogy of literacy instructions; and
- A direct and continuing linkage between initial literacy instruction and post literacy and continuing education.

Activities of rural functional literacy project

- National Literacy Mission envisages an in-built system of autonomy in carrying out functional literacy programmes and activities. Normally, RFLPs are expected to perform the following activities:
- Conduct a detailed survey of the village and mohallas in the project area, prepare socio-economic and cultural profile of the population, plan out a phased programme to ensure total eradication of illiteracy in the project area.
- Identify instructors and other interested adult education workers, select and place them in charge of adult education centres.
- Constitute Project Advisory Committee consisting of representatives of the functionaries, local community, people's organisations, and officials of the concerned development departments.
- Organise learning groups of 30 adult learners and setting up of literacy centres.
- Conduct functional literacy classes.
- Supervise, monitor and evaluate the learners' performance and transit periodical progresses report to the appropriate quarters.
- Arrange training and orientation and orientation programmes for all adult education functionaries.
- Collaborate with different development and welfare agencies for establishing linkage between adult education and the developmental programmes.
- Organised social and cultural programmes and activities like literacy jathas, rallies, fairs and festivals which will promote mass mobilisation and create a climate conducive to literacy learning.
- Co-ordinate the management and functioning of Jan Shikshan Nilayams (JSNs) and Adult Education Center.
- Procure necessary teaching-learning control and maintenance of these materials to the adult literacy centers.

National Literacy Mission

National Literacy Mission (NLM) was set up by the government of India on 5 May 1988 with an aim to eradicate illiteracy in the country by imparting functional literacy to non-literates.

Broad objective

To impart functional literacy to eight crore adult illiterate persons in the age group of 15-35.

Specific objectives

- To make everybody self reliant in the three Rs. 'reading, writing and arithmetic'
- To make them aware of the development issues affecting the society.

Target group

The target group of NLM is people between the ages of 15 and 35. The National Literacy Mission works under the guidance of National the Literacy Mission Authority, an independent wing of Ministry of Human Resources and Development. The National Literacy Mission has two flagship programmes. Total literacy programmes and Post Literacy Programme through which it gives shape to its aims. But with the revitalisation of the National Literacy Mission Programme on 30 September 1999, both the campaigns have come under one single project: 'Literacy Campaigns an Operation Restoration'.

The NLM initiated its first successful literacy campaign in Kottayam city of Kerala followed by Ernakulam district of the same state. Till November 2002, 596 districts out of the total 600 districts of the country had been covered by the National Literacy Mission under the total literacy campaign programme. Out of this, 191 was in the of total literacy campaigns by the National Literacy Mission has achieved due recognitions also. The UN agency-UNESCO in year 1999 conferred upon it UNESCO Noma Literacy Prize. It also received appreciation of the jury for the teaching learning material produced by it and for the voice raised by it to make quality primary education in schools.

In achieving its objective of 100 per cent literacy, the National Literacy Mission takes the help of various NGOs existing across the country. For taking active promotional role in the literacy movement, NGOs are provided financial assistance. The National Literacy Mission also empowers women of the country by including them into their total literacy campaigns. If one goes by the 2001 census, then it will become clear that percentage of female literacy in the country is 54.16. The literacy campaigns undertaken by NLM not only guides females on how to read and write but also make them aware of the various social issues in the society. Through education earned in campaigns by NLM females find themselves tremendously confident. They run their family in a better way and have a greater say in the family matters.

Need and significant of the NLM

The Prime Minister pointed out that one-third of the world's total estimated illiterates would be in India by the turn of the century and this "humiliating" position could be prevented by ensuring the success of the National literacy Mission. The previous programmes of adult education like National Adult Education Programme which was started in 1978 were implemented mostly as government programmes without much involvement of private agencies and public. But no adult education programme has ever succeeded in any country of the world without active support of the people. It has been experienced that little attention was given to upgrading technology for implementing programmes. Despite the thrust on universalisation of primary education and adult education in the past, the total number of illiterates has progressively increased although the percentage of literacy has improved quite well.

A nationwide strategy has been designed for increasing people's awareness and motivation as well as for securing their participation through effective media and communication. Involvement of voluntary agencies in a large number for creating condusive learning environment, for organising mass literacy programmes, for training and technical resource development, experimentations and innovations. A mass movement for literacy should be launched by involving educational institutions, teachers, students, youth, military and Para military personnel, housewives, ex-servicemen, employers, trade unions, etc.

The mechanism for post-literacy and continuing education particularly through establishment of Jana Shikshan Nilayams and better use of existing institutional facilities will be created throughout the country. The institutions/organisations set up for technical resource development at the national, state and district level would ensure production of learning material of good quality.

The National Literacy Mission (NLM) has been conceptualised and built on an objective assessment of the strengths and weaknesses of the earlier programmes emanating from the evaluation study reports. The creation of a mission for literacy presents a national political commitment on the need to harness social forces and channelise the energies of people towards meeting the ultimate objective of effecting qualitative change in their own lives. Conceptually, the mission focuses on:

- A new sense of urgency, seriousness and emphasis with fixed goals, clear time-name and age-specific target groups.
- A firm belief that adults can be made literate according to certain predetermined norms within a stipulated time limit (200 hours) and that it is not too late to learn.
- It emphasizes on the close nexus between literacy of adult parents and enrolment of school going children, on the one hand, and literacy and infant mortality; immunisation and child care on the other.
- A special mission which believes that literacy is not the concern of the one ministry or department or agency but is the concern of the entire nation and all sectors of society.
- It emphasizes on institutionalisation of post-literacy and continuing education in a big way.
- A technology mission also in the sense that besides emphasis on improvement of teaching/learning environment, it lays stress on improvement in the content and process of teaching-learning on a continuing basis.
- It envisages the creation of an effective mission management system to ensure achievement of the mission objectives within a broad framework of flexibility, delegation, decentralisation and accountability.

- It emphasis not on mere enrolment of learners but on attainment of certain predetermined norms and parameters of literacy, numeracy, functionality and awareness.

Strengths

- Women's motivation and participation has been high.
- Coverage of weaker sections of the society (SCs and STs) was higher than the target.
- The project approach to management adopted for adult education programme is feasible.
- The quality of teaching-learning materials prepared bv the National Resource Centre and the State Resource Centers was found to be positive.
- The programme worked well where special recruitment procedures were adopted.

Weaknesses

- The quality of training of the functionaries was poor.
- The learning environment in the adult education centres was poor.
- Mass media did not provide appreciable support. Voluntary agencies did not receive willing cooperation from state governments.
- The existing procedures for their involvement were discouraging.
- There was no linkage between basic literacy, post-literacy, follow-up and continuing education, resulting in the relapse of large number of neo-literates into illiteracy.
- Achievement levels of literacy were below the desired level.
- Training of adult education functionaries at all levels lacked participatory and communicative techniques.
- Political and administrative support of the state governments and the panchayati raj institutions was not forthcoming.

Total Literacy Campaign (TLC)

In the TLC, not only the illiterates in the age group 15-35 are being made literate, but those illiterate children and adults, who do not go to the primary schools are also motivated to attend the non-formal education centers. Apart from this the illiterates above 35 years of age, if interested in education, are given opportunities to become literate; volunteers and workers working in literacy campaigns also try to ensure that all girls and boys in school-going age group get admitted to their nearest primary schools and do not drop out of schools.

Another important programme of TLC is to establish community education centers for neo-literates and for those who happen to leave their studies after third standard for various reasons, to enhance their acquired literacy/education. Normally one community education center is set up for four or five villages or per 5,000 population count. The post-literacy and continuing education programmes for neoliterates have been arranged only third standard for various reasons, to enhance their acquired literacy/education. The children, young and adults all will thus benefit from the literacy campaigns. Every individual will be motivated to become literate and will get the facilities to study further. It is true that the total literacy campaign is not possible by governmental efforts only. Therefore active cooperation and participation is necessary in this endeavour from all groups of people, individuals- only then will this campaign be a success. The real impact of the campaign is best reflected in the census results of 2001, which coincided, with the completion of over a decade of implementation of NLM. According to the census reports the growth of literacy in India during 1981-2001 is as follows:

The increase in literacy between 1981-91 was 8.7 percentage points compared to 12.6 percentage point between 1991-2001. Thus progress during 1991-2001 has been much higher than in earlier decades. With a decline in the absolute number of non - literates from 328 million in 1991 to 304 million in 2001. For the first time educational efforts seem to have overtaken growth in population.

Table 2

	1981	*1991***	*2001*
Population (million)	541.4	688.1	865
Percentage of literacy	43.5	52.2	64.8

* Excludes Assam where 1981 Census not held.

** Excludes Jammu & Kashmir where 1991 census not held.

The country also witnessed a faster growth in female literacy by 14.4 per cent, than that of males, which increased by only 11.13 per cent. The gender gap in literacy, which was 25 per cent in 1991, was reduced to 21.6 per cent in 2001. There is also, for the first time, converging trend in the rural- urban literacy gap. Between 1991 and 2001 rural literacy rates increased by 14 per cent while urban literacy rates increased only by 6.18 per cent thereby reducing the urban-rural gap from 28.39 per cent on 1991 to 21.1 per cent in 2001. However, the most significant rise has been in the rise of literacy rates of the marginalised group like scheduled cast and schedule tribes. The literacy rate of scheduled cast has recorded an increase of 17.3 per cent from 37.4 per cent in 1991 to 54.7 per cent in 2001. Similarly, the literacy rates of scheduled tribes have recorded an increase of 17.5 per cent from 29.6 per cent in 1991 to 47.1 per cent in 2001.

In 1999, before the "Year 2000 Assessment of Education for All", and as part of the ongoing realignment of approach to the literacy movement, NLM began paying special attention to some of the aspects, that later came to be highlighted in the Dakar framework for action. The experience gained form the literacy campaign indicates that substantial number of learners remains outside the ken of literacy activities even after the campaigns due to a variety of reasons. Initially there was no provision for continued or residual illiterate learners. NLM has decided to introduce new strategy to continue the basic teaching learning activities for illiterate learners through transaction of primers and other learning tools even after the campaigns formally came to an end to ensure that the strides made so far are not lost, but consolidated further.

Objectives

The objective of total literacy campaign is to eradicate the illiteracy from the country at the earliest by working at war footing in active participation with all groups and people of society. The main elements of Total Literacy Campaign is as under.

1. Area-based
2. Time-bound
3. Cost-effective
4. Outcome-oriented
5. Voluntary-based

1. *Area-based:* It is expected of all the agencies who wish to manage literacy programmes, that they start their literacy programme only in a specific service area, in the context of a village can be the village, nyana panchayt, development block or the whole district and in the context of a town a mohalla, ward or the town itself. The service area will be chosen by the agency, in view of its capability, strength and available resources and depending on its rapport with the local community. The service area should be chosen in consultation with such workers and officers who have been entrusted with co-ordination work. Total literacy campaigns are generally co-ordinate by the District Magistrate or District adult education officer. The selected service area should be made compact and continuous and no colony or circle should be left out.
2. *Time-bound:* The agencies connected with TLC should specially keep in mind that they need to work in a selected service-area for a very long period. The service area should be saturated in a timebound manner. It will be proper if it is planned for two years. It can be up to three years maximum.
3. *Cost-effectiveness:* The TLC is planned to provide functional literacy to the maximum number of illiterates incurring minimum expenditure. Literacy experts, adult educationalists, planning experts and administrators have kept a provision of Rs. 65.00 to Rs. 100.00 to make an illiterate, literate. It is worth mentioning that the financial provision is not based on the number of registered

illiterates but the above said provision is based on the number of persons made literate.

4. *Outcome-oriented:* In TLC, more stress is laid on the achievement instead of registration. The previous literacy programmes have paid more attention to registration. The number of adult learners who could achieve national literacy norms, was given lesser consideration. TLC is totally result-oriented.
5. *Volunteer-based:* The TLC is mostly volunteer based. The success of this literacy campaign depends mainly on the volunteer teachers. He lives amongst the illiterates he has to educate. Most of the time he will motivate them to learn. The more the volunteer is capable of explaining to them, inspiring them, the more will be the success of the campaigning. The most important thing is that only the volunteer teacher will make the people literate. Though the volunteer will not get any salary or honorarium, yet he will surely get respect, honour and fame. It is said that "to impart education is the biggest charity." This charity is being done by the volunteer teacher in the TLC and hence he is the one to be facilitated and rewarded.

Role of Jana Shikshan Nilayam (JSN)

It is believed that Neo-literates tend to forget what they learnt. JSN was established in February 1988 and enables learners to continue their learning beyond elementary literacy. JSN includes programmes to be organised as a part of farmers training programme rural radio forum, charchamandal, etc. Efforts are being made to steer the development process towards weaker section of society. Basic objective in planning was to ensure retention of literacy skills, other facilities for learners to learn beyond their elementary literacy. Prerak is identified and he is In-charge of JSN.

Objectives of JSN

- Provision of facilities for literacy
- Dissemination of information to the beneficiaries
- Creation of awareness among illiterates

- Improvement of economic conditions of the beneficiaries
- Recreation and healthy living of the poor and illiterate masses.

Functions of JSN

- Organising of evening classes.
- Library
- Reading room
- Charchamandal
- Short term training programmes
  - Health and family welfare
  - Development in agriculture and animal husbandry
  - Conservation of energy
  - Improved chula.

Structure of Administration

- JSNs are established as permanent continuing education centres.
- They serve a population of about 5,000 spread over cluster of four-five contiguous villages.
- Established on a priority basis.
  - Schools building
  - Panchayat ghar
  - Other public buildings, etc.
- Agencies organising the functional literacy programmes are also operating JSNs.
- Area of operation of basic literacy programme is shifted in due course. The DAEO and one of the APOs from the project to be designated as APOs (JSN).
- Voluntary agencies or other agencies, the JSNs in that area will look after by the concerned agency.

Shramik Vidhapeeths

The scheme of SVP is a special programme in adult education for deprived section of society. The scheme is in operation since 1967, fully funded by Government of India.

- The Government expanded the scheme
  1. Polyvalent approach
  2. Programme designed to suit the learners
  3. Inter-disciplinary approach
  4. Utilisation of resources
  5. Flexibility in organising courses.
- The Polyvalent Approach includes: -
  - Various learning needs of participation
  - Programmes designed for speciallv homogeneous target group.
  - Need-base courses rather than offering pre-designed course content
  - Courses such as:
    - Health & hygiene
    - Sanitation
    - Communication
- The management:
  - Functions as autonomous organisations under:
    - Registered voluntary agencies
    - State governments
    - Universities
- Is managed by a board of management that inclues:
  - Members representing the interest of workers
  - Employees
  - Educational members
  - Training the deprived sections of society
- The Target includes:
  - Socio-economically and educational backward and disadvantaged group of urban population:
    - Men
    - Youth
    - Women
    - Self employed

- Employed
- Priority is given to:
  - Illiterates
  - Semi literates
  - Skilled
  - Semi skilled
  - SC/ST girls/women
  - Working children & school drop out.

Basic Features

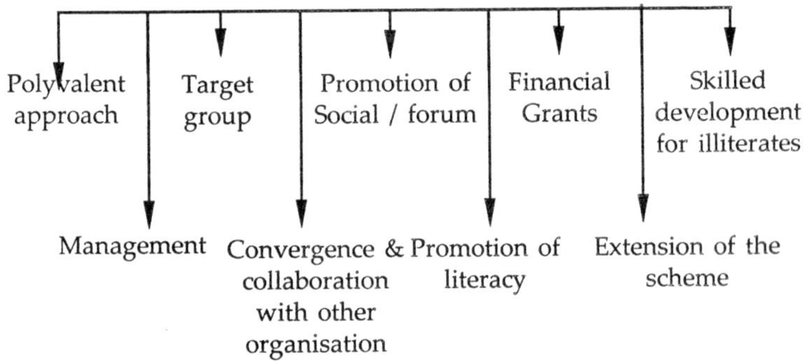

- There is convergence and collaboration with other agencies:
  - Welfare centre
  - Development agencies
  - Financial institution, etc.

Promotion of Societies / Forums

Forums like mahilamandal, yuvakmandals, cooperative, cultural and sports club, etc., have helped in seeking participation and have benefited the target groups in undertaking economic, social and cultural and welfare activities, which have raised their income and standard of living

Promotion of literacy

Objectives of NLM, SVPs were also geared up to participate actively in promotion of literacy in respective areas of operation.

Skilled development for illiterates

Programme evolving technical vocational skills to design appropriate course for more Involvement of illiterates.

State resource centre (SRC)

It is recognised as management tool but its entry in the field of education that is adult education has been late. Systematic attempts in this direction began in 1976 and achieved measures of success In 1978 it was considered to have an institution in every state and should providing technical support.

Functions Performed by SRCs

1. Curriculum development and preparation of teaching and learning materials of methodological guidelines.
2. Training of project officers and supervisors, resource person.
3. Post literacy and follow-up material.
4. Assistance in environment building through mass media publication of posters etc.

The needs of the learners were identified in the context of the literacy, functionally and awareness aspects.

- The cycle library were used and it proved to be successful.
- Priority was given on teaching learning materials and to training, organising relevant programmes and activities.

UNESCO

1. UNESCO is also interested in promoting adult literacy both as a human right and as an instrument of liberation and development.
2. It undertook a large-scale experimental world literacy programme (EWLP). Its contribution was to test functional literacy and work oriented literacy.

3. It was clear that selective approach of EWLP by itself was not enough.

Table 4: Literacy Status in Nine most Populous Countires

Country	*Total Non-literate Population 15+ age*	*Literacy Rate 15+ (%)*		
		Total	*Male*	*Female*
Mexico	6.52	91	92	90
Indonesia	15.10	90	94	87
Brazil	17.36	89	88	89
China	87.01	91	95	87
Nigeria	—	—	—	—
India	268.42	61	73	48
Egypt	14.21	71	83	59
Pakistan	48.81	50	63	36
Bangladesh	52.53	43	52	33

Source: Education for All-Global Monitoring Report - 2007

Table 5: Literacy Rate 1951-2001

Census Year	*Persons*	*Male*	*Female*
1951	18.33	27.16	8.86
1961	28.30	40.40	15.35
1971	34.45	45.96	21.97
1981	43.57	56.38	29.76
1991	52.21	64.13	39.29
2001	64.84	75.26	53.67

Literacy Scenario in India (As per 2001 Census)

Literacy in India has made remarkable strides since Independence. This has been further confirmed by the results of the Census 2001. The literacy rate has increased from 18.33 per cent in 1951 to 64.84 per cent in 2001. This is despite the fact that during the major part of the last five decades there has been exponential growth of the population at nearly 2% per annum.

Table 6: Other Asian Countries

Country	*Total Non-literate Population 15+ age (in million)*	*Literacy Rate 15+ (%) (2000)*		
		Total	*Male*	*Female*
Thailand	3.35	93	95	91
Philippines	3.50	93	93	93
Vietnam	4.90	90	94	87
Malaysia	1.72	89	92	85
Indonesia	15.10	90	94	87
China	87.01	91	95	87
Myanmar	3.20	90	94	86
Iran	10.50	77	84	70
Laos	1.01	69	77	61
Afghanistan	9.04	28	43	13

Source: Education for All-Global Monitoring Report - 2007

Some of the important highlights of Census 2001 are given below:

1. The literacy rate in the country has increased to 64.84%, which reflects an overall increase of 12.63%, the fastest decadal growth ever. This is the highest rate since independence.
2. The male literacy rate has increased to 75.26%, which shows an increase of 11.13%. On the other hand, the female literacy of 53.67% has increased at a much faster rate of 14.38%.
3. The male-female literacy gap has reduced from 24.84% in 1991 to 21.59% in 2001 Mizoram has the smallest gap (3.97%) followed by Kerala (6.52%) and Meghalaya (5.82%).
4. All states and union territories without exception have shown increase in literacy rates during 1991-2001.
5. In all the states and union territories the male literacy rate except Bihar (59.68%) is now over 60%.

6. For the first time since independence there has been a decline in the absolute number of illiterates during the decade. In the previous decades, there has been a continuous increase in the number of illiterates, despite the increase in the literacy rates, but now for the first time the total number of illiterates has come down by 24.77 million.
7. The number of literate persons has increased to 560.68 million in 2001 thus adding an additional 201.40 million literates in the country.
8. Rajasthan has recorded the highest increase i.e.21.86% in the literacy rate among the states/UTs of India. Literacy rate of Rajasthan in 7+ population in 1991 was 38.55% which has increased to 60.41% in 2001.
9. The state also recorded very good increase in the female literacy. It was 20.44% in 1991, which has increased to 43.85% in 2001.
10. The female literacy rate of Chhattisgarh in 7+ population in 1991 was 27.52% which has increased to 51.85% in 2001. Thus the rise in female literacy rate in Chhattisgarh has been to the extent of 24.33%, which is the highest among all the states/UTs of the country.
11. Madhya Pradesh also recorded a good increase in female literacy rate, i.e. 20.94%. In 1991 the literacy rate of females was 29.35%, which has increased to 50.29% in 2001.

Need and Significance of Adult Education

Adult education is an impelling need; the need is so imperative and over-powering that all men and women must be helped to acquire the skills and knowledge that would enable them to properly fit into the society which is fast moving. An illiterate person will face innumerable hurdles in this scientific and rapidly changing world of cutthroat competition. Literacy is not only a means of liberation but also an instrument of social change. It is a tool for acquiring and sharing information on national development. Economic recession and growing burden of debt have no doubt played a major role in decline of basic education. Literacy increases peoples' capacity to cope with the demands of living and working. Adult education is a tool to influence human thinking in a right direction. Infact, development of society depends primarily on the quality and effectiveness of its people. The importance of adult education for human resource development is being seriously recognised which is imperative for the economic development as well as for strengthening the base of democracy. The significance of universal literacy as an instrument of galvanising and mobilising the people, arousing community consciousness and community participation for bringing about social change.

Education is a life long process. It is essential for each and every individual because it helps in building the character and modifying the behaviour of an individual according to the needs and environment of a society. Education is an instrument of social change and development. It is most important in achieving the rapid development and technological progress. Education should not be restricted to a few years of life; instead it should be a life long education so that it could widen the interests of educated person in variety of ways. The contemporary knowledge explosion changes the volume and content or knowledge so fast that the knowledge acquired during any period of life becomes incomplete and outdated. So in order to have uptodate knowledge one needs to continue to learn during the adult years also. There are millions of people, who have not been able to acquire even the necessary minimum of education during their childhood because of the economic circumstances of their families. They are, therefore, faced to live unfulfilled lives at low level of income, social states and awareness. There must be some provision for them to acquire in later life the knowledge which they could not acquire in youth. Therefore the organisation of further education for adults become more important.

Adult education should mean the special type of education for adults above the age of 18 years, who either did not receive any education in their early life or could not extend their early literacy by taking the advantage of the educational institutions. Hadler (1970) defines it as: "Adult education Is a process through which persons no longer attending school as a regular, fulltime basis undertake activities with the conscious intention of bringing about change in information, knowledge, understanding, skills, appreciation and attitude." In the modern world, the role of a woman goes much beyond the hone and bringing up of children. She has to play her role as individual, a citizen and member of society, a homemaker and active participant in socio--political and psycho-physio environment. These roles of a woman has affected the art of home making also. In the past, home making education to the girls was given by the elder female member of the family, but now because of the nuclear family pattern it is not possible. Due to technological developments, home making has also become complicated. The human needs are also changing rapidly as the standard of living and society are developing. So education is necessary to acquire the knowledge of art of home making. Secondly, rapid urbanisation is forcing people to shift from the rural area to the urban area in search of employment and better life. So it becomes necessary to help the immigrants to adopt themselves to the environment of urban setting.

Non-formal education is one of the major educational innovations of the modern times which is not only trying to meet the educational needs of the uneducated who have not been able to acquire formal education, but also to meet the demands of the modern society by equipping the people with uptodate knowledge. It is intended for all — illiterate, semiliterate and literate; youth and adults; working men and women and urban and rural people. Non-formal education for adults is important as this is remedial education through which mature individuals and mature society can be prepared. Adult education by its very nature is non-formal in character. It is out of school education meeting the educa-tional needs of the adults.

Sharma (1977) has said, "When you teach a man, you teach an-individual, but when you teach a woman, you teach a nation." Therefore, to improve the standard of living of the weaker sections, it becomes important to educate the adult women and to give them economic freedom. In India, more preference is given to educate the men as compared to that of women. When the weaker sections are not able to educate their men, it is unthinkable for them to educate their women. So the educational programmes should be centred around the needs of the adult women who belong to the weaker sections of the society.

Nowadays in almost all the states of India, different institutions and organisations have started to run adult education classes for the women. Adult education programmes are being carried on by the social organisations, corporations, unions, governmental agencies and educational institutions in Baroda for women from the weakers sections of Baroda city. Non-formal educational system is not rigid and formal in its nature. The curriculum is based on the felt needs and interests of the people. If needed, education will go to the community, but the community will not be expected to come to the institutions and stay for a limited period of time with the fixed periods of entry and exit. The non-formal educational institutions may not have enough funds to spend *on* good teaching materials and facilities as unlike the formal institutions, they either provide free education or charge very nominal fees. So the problems faced by the non-formal education programmes would be different from the formal education programmes. One of the major factors in the success of any development programme is its proper implementation. However good a plan of action of a programme may be, there are always problems faced in its execution. It is important to know their problems and emphasise should be given to the solution of these problems for the success of the programmes.

Moreover, there have been several studies done to know the extent of participation; reasons of attending and not attending the adult education classes; attitudes of adults towards adult education classes; educational needs, interests and worries of adults. But the important area of research, regarding the teachers and the organisers of the adult education programmes, has not been explored. There are hardly any studies on the problems of the teachers and the organisers of adult education programmes in imparting non-formal adult education, they may come across several problems. These problems may be regarding motivation, teaching methods and aids, physical facilities and evaluation According to the UNESCO the term adult education denotes the entire body of organised educational processes, whatever the content level and method, whether they prolong or replace initial education in schools, colleges, as well as apprenticeship. Thereby persons regarded as adults by the society to which they belong develops their abilities, enrich their knowledge, improve their technical or professional qualification and bring about changes in their attitude or behaviour in the twofold perspectives of full personal development and participation in a balanced and independent social, economic and cultural development.

Adult education programme as envisaged in the national adult education programme is meant primarily for women and learners belonging to deprived section of the population. This does not mean that others willing to join adult education programme should be excluded, but emphasis must be given to this section of the population for they constitute about 60 to 70 per cent of India's population which did not have the benefit of any type of education formal or informal. The relationship between literacy and social development is mediated by the role, spread and quality of education. The problem of adequate socioeconomic development has both an individual and a collective/ social dimension, being a problem not only for the individual but also for society as a whole. Greater literacy in some cases may mean greater/ better opportunities for socio-economic improvement in individual lives/families, without much impact on other factors.

Mass poverty, especially, cannot be resolved by treating it as a sum of individual problems to be resolved individually. It must be seen as a collective problem requiring collective solutions. Mass literacy, on the other hand, because of the criticality of its size and pressure, may set off certain chain reactions, on the socioeconomic, and political -administrative structures, the evidence of which we found in many areas. But it cannot by itself resolve the collective problem of mass-scale impoverishment or widening inequalities in socioeconomic conditions. In the absence of collective solutions of these problems, it is extremely difficult to either stabilise newly acquired literacy skills, or set off the spiral movement for social development discussed above.

Precisely because basic or minimal literacy is not basic or minimal education, it is not "sticky downwards". That is to say, it has no natural or intrinsic propensity to being cumulative or stable. Literacy is a training or skill whose purpose and value is contingent upon the availability of opportunities for its use, and upon benefits, economic, politico-social and cultural, to be derived from its use. The functionality dimension of literacy in India remains a problematic area. Almost as serious a problem as the lack of widespread literacy is the fragility of literacy achievements and the phenomenon of relapse of former neo-literates.

Recent researches in the developing countries of the Asia-Pacific region reveal that ignorance among the poor in rural areas in particular about many aspects of the physical and social world around them, has mainly arisen from lack of access to information due to literacy.

The poor, especially the women, have very little knowledge about various essential elements like health, nutrition, credit and saving, use of new technology for agriculture, animal husbandry, legal rights, various poverty alleviation programmes, etc.

The economists thus feel that out of several reasons, literacy is the major cause for poverty. Education plays a very important role in attacking on poverty and enhancing the quality of life. It is being recognised that there is a need to build and strengthen the national capacities of the member states, providing support for regional networking and for identifying innovative integrated approaches to literacy for poverty alleviation.

The current literacy and continuing education programmes are looked upon educational programmes that address poverty concerns. The UNESCO (Japanese fund trust) have taken up the project which is the inter-country initiative and includes six countries (China, India, Indonesia, Maldives, Mongolia and Nepal). They had set some objectives for the same which are as follows:

General objective

To strengthen personnel and institutional at the regional, national and sub national levels in policy formulation, planning, management, monitoring and evaluation of functional literacy programmes for poverty alleviation.

Specific objectives

- To present an analytical description of national initiative in the area of adult education in India.
- To analyse and identity the specific references to poverty in the approach, content and coverage of the adult literacy programme of the India.

- To present an analytical case study of a Literacy Campaign in India, dealing with poverty and development issues through literacy.
- To draw lessons from the Literacy Campaign Case Study for sharing with other countries.

The reasons are:

- acquiring a new skill is itself a source of greater self worth.
- literacy is an empowering skill which reduces many fears, of being lost, cheated, manipulated by others. It also increases access to many types of information that one needs/wants to achieve a more satisfying life, to carry out one's responsibilities more efficiently/effectively, even to challenge/reject, if necessary what has been learnt through one's socialisation in an unequal society. It thus provides the potential (but not the guarantee) for a better life politically, culturally socially and economically.

Social development should not be confused with economic development nor with socioeconomic development. Socioeconomic development can be understood for our purposes here as a socially humane and equitable form of economic development. Social development is a wider concept encompassing the latter two terms. It is akin to the striving for "the good society", for which the learning process, of constant enrichment of that process, is an essential and integral element, along with effective, responsible and willing participation and the achievement of a more equitable order. A dynamic and virtuous spiral can then be established. A better society or better social development leads to better education which leads to better social development, and further improvement of educational opportunities and quality, which in turn improves the prospect of better social development, etc.

A minimum level, and equitable distribution of socioeconomic development is necessary to eradicate hunger, chronic poverty, undernourishment, malnourishment, permanent indebtedness—which fuel exploitation, powerlessness, dependency and inequality. There must also be access to basic health care and security/shelter i.e. the minimum conditions for decent physical existence must be established for this qualitative leap in the educational-social development spiral to take off. These, together with complete literacy, are in any case envisaged in the Directive Principles of State Policy in the Constitution of the Indian Republic. To achieve this stage, however, education itself has to play a far more active, participatory and dynamic role, to provide the motive, the rationale, the skills, the values and the vision of what is meant by a better society. At the moment, India is still very far from approaching that level of social development. The inadequacies, inequities and maladies of the educational process are both a cause and effect of this situation.

Role of 'Pragati Centre' in Empowering Women

The Department of Home Science Extension and Communication was started in 1953 with one of the objective to develop abilities in conducting and evaluating urban and rural non-formal education programme to meet the national needs. The aims of these programmes are:

1. To offer the programme, which is based on the local, needs of the urban community.
2. To offer the programme to the educational and economically deprived groups of urban community.
3. To provide the opportunities to adult women for intellectual, aesthetic and vocational development.
4. To offer opportunities for the development of creativity among children, adolescent girls and adult women for their vocational development.
5. To create interest in income generating activities among young girls and adult women.

Non-formal education and adult education programmes are conducted every year in the different urban and rural communities. The Department of Home Science Extension and Communication had resources and expertise available, but it was difficult to conduct the adult education programme because of the shortage of infrastructure facilities. On the other side it was difficult to contact new target group every year and lot of time was wasted in building up rapport with the different target groups in the different communities. So, it was decided that let the women come to the Department of Home Science Extension and Communication for the adult education programme where the adult education classes could be conducted in a most effective manner as different teaching aids, different teaching methods, television, video, tape recorder can be used very conveniently by the adult educators.

Then, 'Pragati' was started in 1983 for conducting the adult education programme in the Department of Home Science Extension and Communication. 'Pragati' is one of the precious possessions of the Department of Home Science Extension and Communication. It is the path towards the building of the women's skills, thoughts and new ideas. It also brings the light of awareness to the women. All the facilities are provided in its centre like electricity, furniture, gas, washbasin etc. It was inaugurated on 2 September 1997 by Shri S. C. Jetley, Regional Director of ONGC, Baroda, with the great effort of the Home Science Extension and Communication staff, Alumni Association of the Department and many great donors. It is a place where the undergraduates' students under the supervision of the teachers conduct adult education classes. On one hand, the aim of the 'Pragati' centre is to make the women empowered by bringing out the girls and women from their home and engage them into the educational, recreational and productive arts and crafts activities so as to get new knowledge and ideas which can help in changing their behaviour and attitude, develop their personality and skills.

On the other hand, it helps in the professional development of the third-year students by providing the training to plan, organise and conduct the adult education programme. If one assumes that every year about 100 adult women attended the adult education programme and 40 adult educators were trained for last 50 years, so, it can be said that the Department of Home Science Extension and Communication has helped 5,000 women to be empowered and 2,000 adult educators were trained.

In order to conduct the adult education programme in the Department of Home Science Extension and Communication, it was decided to contact Baroda Municipal Corporation and its Urban Basic Service (UBS) Urban Community Development, (UCD) community volunteers to bring the adult learners to the Department of Home Science Extension and Communication as they also have more or less similar objectives, i.e., to encourage and guide socially and economically backward urban people to participate in the programme of their upliftment, promote equality and improve social and the physical condition as they have the projects like literacy programme, nutrition and income generating programme etc.

In 'Pragati Centre' the adult educators demonstrate different nutritious and delicious recipes and they deal with the different topics like dowry, health education, literacy, reproductive health, environment education, consumer education, women's right, women's empowerment, income generation, etc., with the use of different methods like demonstration, workshop, discussion, puppet show, drama, educational talk etc and materials like charts, posters, puppets, flash cards, flipcharts, films, slides, models, specimens, diagrams, etc. Women take active part in each activity. Here opportunities are given to women to express their views on important family matters, on their education, marriage and employment. There by it changes their attitude and different patterns of role sets, which may be quite different from that of their traditional roles. It is rightly said that self-sufficiency is the 'key to stronger women'. Many of the problems, which are faced by women, existed because they were either illiterate or economically dependent on others. With a view to creating a climate where women are expected and treated as equals, it is extremely important to ensure a comprehensive curriculum for adult education programme.

Devadas (1979) mentioned that the report of the Committee on the Status of Women in India (1974) emphasised the need for constitution and legal guarantee in changing the lives of the vast majority of Indian women who do not have the knowledge to improve their conditions of living. Therefore, adult education programmes for women are needed to make them conscious of their rights and responsibilities, assist them to acquire economic freedom, provide them with excess to the knowledge and skills needed in day-to-day living, particularly in the areas of health, childcare, nutrition, management of resources and better family living, and to strengthen their participation in the total development process.

The weaker sections form a major part of our country's population. Bhatty (1976) mentions five poverty lines derived by the different standards as Rs. 180, 240, 300, 360 and 420 per person per year. He also notes that four-fifths of the population in each of the states—Gujarat, Tamil Nadu, Madhya Pradesh, Rajasthan, Orissa—is below the poverty line of Rs.360 per year. It shows that a major part of our country's population lives in unthinkable poverty. They are not able to afford formal education with very little income at their disposal. Also the formal education is inadequate or irrelevant to solve their basic problems.

The history of the movement for improving women's status all over the world and especially in India shows emphasis from the beginning on education as the most significant instrument for changing women's subjugated position in society. Increase of educational and opportunities and the removal of traditional barriers on entry of women to particular branches and levels of educations, came to be supported by champions of women's emancipation from the nineteenth century onwards. Social reformers in India emphasized the crucial importance of education of women to improve their status in society. According to the reformers, the main purpose for education of women was not to make them more efficient and active units in the process of socio-economic or political development, but to make them more capable of fulfilling their traditional roles in society as wives and mothers.

Education for women was regarded as a means to improve their status within the family, and not to equip them to play any economic role in the wider social context. According to R.C.Majumdar, the absence of any economic compulsion was, in fact, the main reason for the slow progress of women's education in this country. Because of their reluctance to interfere in social matters, the colonial authorities generally supported the purely humanitarian and a limited view of women's education. The emphasize on education equipping women to carry out their multiple roles as citizens, housewives, mothers, contributors to the family income and builders of the new society helped as choice ingredient for the improvement of their status.

The National Committee on Women's Education had reviewed the progress of women's education before, during and after Independence and concluded that in spite of the direct action taken by the states for this purpose after independence, "the education of women has not made satisfactory progress between 1947 and 57." But one must comment on the change of situation in later years. For women's education as social institution has developed certain convictions for the society. Anderson and Parker mention some important educational convictions of the American society, and they are applicable to Indian society as it is developing on the American model to an extent. Among these conviction the first is:

i) *Education can solve problems:* The underlying conviction in America is that education is a cure-all that can solve most of the social problems of our society and lead the way to human betterment.

ii) *Education for all:* A third conviction which has been a symbol of our democratic society is that opportunity to obtain education should be equal to all. (Anderson and Parker, 1964. In spite of this education for women has been lagging behind).

Lately we have noticed that women have entered high skilled jobs in information technology in developing countries. This has happened particularly in countries where national policies have promoted science technology education and where young women entered these fields in many cases in percentages far greater than in developed countries. In India, women occupy nearly 20 per cent of the professional jobs in the software industry, with higher percentages found in Calcutta and Bangalore. However, nowhere are these jobs the majority of those held by women in the workforce nor are women the majority of workers in these occupations. The workings in these areas comprise small, educated elite. However, it is an important area for women to break into and become role models for the next generation whose numbers in these fields are likely to increase. The advent technology of information technology in globalisation has brought changes in the location of work. These are the major aspects to the spatial re-organisation of women's work under the impact of information technologies in developing countries: home-based work and teleworking. Women who have lost their formal sector manufacturing jobs frequently turn to this less desirable jobs to remain in the labour force. This phenomenon is often referred as the casualisation of labour. These jobs frequently take place in the home. In developing countries, while information technology has created many new jobs for women, with advancing technology, women have lost many of those created in the first wave of industrialisation and are finding fewer new jobs in the second wave of computer-aided manufacturing and services. Many young women are doing jobs previously done by men and taking places in new fields of work created by developments and technologies. More young women in developing countries are going out in search of job. As information technology become more tightly linked with development of knowledge economics, education and training for young women become more and more important.

Female literacy in science and technology is crucial for social and economic development. Education and access to technological and scientific know-how is a key factor to sustainable development globally and significant tool for social change and progress in everyday life. Market oriented arguments in the context of competition; global market economy and the need for creativity also provide a compelling justification for women's inclusion in the sciences. Within the logics of competitive society today, the exclusion of female talent, potential and creativity represents an inadmissible of underutilisation of talent, creativity and human resources in society.

Economic empowerment of women is fundamental to their overall empowerment. It implies a better quality of material life through sustainable livelihoods, owned and managed by women. In a country like India, where the gender divide and the equalities between men and women is so wide, providing the skill and the opportunity to economically self-sufficient must go hand in hand with social and political empowerment. Helping women to organise themselves into Self-Help Groups (SHGs) and helping them again access to micro credit and undertake income generating activities, are important ways to achieve the goal of economic empowerment. It has been found to be an effective strategy that caters to the needs and gender reality of women. Today, SHGs are to be found in rural as well as urban areas. They work on range of issue which apart from income generation activities and micro-credit also includes health, nutrition, agriculture, forestry, etc.

Distance education and its associated technologies allow us to increase to education and provide a quality of education which is otherwise often not possible through traditional means. Two important dimensions of technology being used are affordability and appropriateness for rural women. The technologies should be views as the 'tools of the trade' rather than the driving force behind education. It has been reiterated by number of authors based on several research studies that each medium has its own strengths and limitations. No medium is superior, and often a combination of media can be more effective. Selection of appropriate media is an important factor in reaching out the specific target groups. The alternatives media, visually reach small booklets with little text, flip charts, posters, traditional media have been imaginatively used by NGOs in generating awareness on women's empowerment and women's rights as well.

In short, women empowerment is an ongoing and dynamic process, which enhances women's ability to change those structures and ideologies that keep them subordinate. This process enables then to gain more access to resources and decision making, more control over their own lives and greater autonomy. Empowerment is a process that changes and improves women's self-image and social image, and enables women to challenge and change not just hierarchical gender relation, but all hierarchical and inqualitable relations in society. Women's struggles and movements, peasants and workers movements human rights movements, and movements for democratisation and decentralisation of society. Women empowerment is not a one-away process, where some activists and experts can go and empower other. It is a multidimensional and integrative process, an ongoing journey, where there are several milestones:

a) Making women's contribution to the society visible.
b) Affirming women 's knowledge, skills and experience in other areas.
c) Creating a social environment that gives women self-esteem and self-confidence

d) Providing opportunities for empowerment, education to girls and women and providing support to them to move into non-traditional roles and take decisions about themselves.

e) Enhancing women's participation in processes at all levels.

f) Making facilities and resources available and accessible.

g) Enabling women to gain access to and control over means of production, property and other resources and over their own labour, income, bodies and sexuality.

Thus, the question of illiteracy among women is closely related to the question of educational deprivation among the women in general. Many reasons can be responsible for this.

In the modern world, the role of a woman goes much beyond the home and bringing up of children. She has to play her role as individual, a citizen and member of society, a home maker and active participant in socio-political and psycho-physical environment. These roles of a woman has affected the art of home making also. In the past, home making education to the girls was given by the elder female member of the family, but now because of the nuclear family pattern it is not possible. Due to technological developments, home making has also become complicated. The human needs are also changing rapidly as the standard of living and society are developing. A greater number of man made and scientific devices are coming into the existence. So education is necessary to acquire the knowledge of art of home making. Secondly, rapid urbanisation is forcing people to shift from the rural area to the urban area in search of employment and better life. So it becomes necessary to help the immigrants to adapt themselves to the environment of urban life as the urban life is based on technology for most of the activities and processes which are associated with modernity and economic problems. Mostly the weaker sections of the society do not get the opportunity to continue their early literacy. So the programmes should be centered around the need of adults who belong to the poor section of the society.

Empowerment implies the creation of an enabling environment where individuals can fully use their capabilities to take charge of their lives. Empowerment also implies the building or acquiring of capacity to accomplish certain tasks and attain specific goals. In the areas of women's political empowerment, it is increasingly becoming recognised that women should both empower themselves and 'be empowered'. This relates both to individual and collective empowerment. Empowerment also involves creating a conducive environment so that women can use these competencies to address the fundamental problems of society on par with their male counterparts. It follows therefore that building the analytical, political, advocacy, leadership, networking and other competencies of women is just as important as or even more important than increasing women's numbers in high policy and decision making bodies and institutions.

These qualitative factors provide the foundation for sustainable improvements in the position of women. Otherwise legislative or constitutional mandates may merely result in tokenism, manipulation and unsustainable representation. Moreover, indicators of true empowerment should show that increasingly women are breaking traditional boundaries and stereotypes, this can happen only by spreading of education.

Need for Evaluating the Adult Education Programme

Much of the success of the adult education programme will depend upon the manner in which it is implemented and evaluated. Evaluation is an integral part of the adult education programme of 'Pragati Centre'. It must be continuous process starting from the planning stage and follow-up stage. Evaluation of the adult education programme of 'Pragati Centre' is necessary not only for assessing the level of achievement of the learners but also to aid and accelerate the pace of their learning. Evaluation is an important process to know the success and failure of the programme. It may be difficult to evaluate the non-formal education programmes, as formal evaluation techniques can not be used for evaluation. There is absence of established evaluation principles. In a formal education programme, formal evaluation techniques are used. In non-formal education programme, the women may not like to be evaluated. It may be difficult to evaluate due to irregularity of attendance of the women in the classes. The organisers may not be having the progress reports of any other programme with which to compare and evaluate their own programmes. It may be difficult to evaluate the adult women by observation.

Evaluation is a complementary process. The aim of evaluating the adult education programme of 'Pragati Centre' is to improve the programme and also helps in giving future direction. An effort is being made to introduce a process-oriented continuous evaluation system that will help for checking carefully the different aspect of the programme of 'Pragati Centre', which is essential for bringing about the improvement in the quality and efficacy in the Adult Education programme. In order to be suitable and effective the adult education programme needs to be evaluated from time to time. So, the investigator has undertaken a study of an appraisal of adult education programme of 'Pragati Centre' of the Department of Home Science Extension and Communication. Faculty of Home Science

Statement of the Problem

Looking at the above scenario of adult education programme it was decided to take up a study on "An appraisal of adult education programme of 'Pragati Centre' of the Department of Home Science Extension and Communication, Faculty of Home Science, The M.S.University, Baroda in the year 2003-2004. Gujarat.

Justification of the Study

The success and the failure of any programme depend upon how it is planned and implemented. The job is not over after the execution of any programme, one has to evaluate its efficiency and achievements by checking to what extent the programme is able to accomplish its goal. The following are the major points, which justify the study in the Department of Home Science Extension and Communication.

Improvement of the Programme

The Adult Education Programme is being run by the Department of Home Science Extension and Communication for more than 50 years. Much of the time, efforts and money have been spent by the adult educators as well as the supervisors in conducting the adult education programme. There is a need to know the strength of the Adult Education Programme so that educators can continue with the same in the future also and to make special efforts to remove the weaknesses, which are the barriers in the success of the adult education programme, thus making the programme more stronger and efficient.

Third year students conduct the adult education programme in 'Pragati Centre' under the guidance of teacher supervisors of the Department of Home Science Extension and Communication who help them in planning the Adult Education Programme. Supervisors conduct meetings and discussions for the improvement of the Adult Education Programme keeping in mind the adult learners' interest, needs and problems. Efforts can be put in while planning the programme for better implementation in future.

Usefulness of Data

The systematic study of evaluation of aduit education programme will provide authentic data, which can be presented to the University Grant Commission who are the policy makers, which will provide a base to show the problems in conducting the adult education programme, reasons for irregularity in attendance. The data can be useful to the undergraduate students as they can get an idea about the adult learners that what they have already learnt? What changes they want in the adult education classes? What are the new things they want to add? What are their demands, needs and problems?

Proper Utilisation of Funds

The Department of Home Science Extension and Communication is providing sufficient funds for the implementation of the Adult Education Programme to educate the adult learners, like giving contingency money for conducting demonstrations, workshops, dramas, expert talks and arranging educational trips. So, it is essential to evaluate whether proper utilisation of these funds is being done or not, whether its objectives of social, economical and political awareness have been met or not. For the non-formal education, which is for children or school dropouts, instructors go to the communities and conduct the programme but in case of the adult education programme the adult learners come to the 'Pragati Centre' of the Department of Home Science Extension and Communication to attend the adult education classes. They might be facing the problem of transportation, and many times they may not be getting the bus on time or it may be expensive for them to come by an autorickshaw. The adult learners may not be aware about the time, place where the classes are conducted or they may have to look after the family members. So, the study will be helpful in understanding the problems or reasons for not attending the adult education classes regularly.

Follow-up of the Programme

The Adult Education Programme conducted in 'Pragati Centre' aims at empowering women. This study will be helpful in knowing whether the women have really gained the knowledge and applied it in their life or just came in the programme for the sake of attending the adult education classes.

Suggestions

The Adult Education Programme conducted in 'Pragati Centre' may not be according to the needs and interests of the adult learners so, it may be possible that adult learners have some different needs, wants and interests. This programme is conducted for the adult learners so it is very necessary that the topics, which are covered, are according to their needs and interests. The suggestions of the adult learners will provide a base to the adult educators and supervisors for better planning and implementation of the adult education programme in future. The suggestions of the Adult learners will contribute in making a more effective Adult Education Programme in the Department of Home Science Extension and Communication.

Suggestions from the supervisors and Urban Basic Services and Urban Community Development Project's Community Volunteers are also very important. The teacher supervisors help in planning and guiding the adult educators to conduct the adult education programme, and UBS/UCD community volunteers help in bringing the adult learners in the 'Pragati Centre' from the different urban slum communities of Baroda. Many studies have been conducted in the other states but no specific study has been conducted in the Department of Home Science Extension and Communication on the evaluation of adult education programme of 'Pragati Centre'. So, there is a need to evaluate the adult education programme.

Justification of the Variables

Age

The adults of the younger age group may have different opinions regarding the Adult Education Programme as they may be more enthusiastic and interested in the adult education programme in comparison to the adults of the older age group. The older people are rigid and stick to their knowledge.

The adults of the older age group may opine that they are not much interested in discussing about the issues like reproductive health, family planning, etc., whereas, the younger people like to have changes in life so, the adults of the younger age group may opine that they want to learn some new ideas like best out of waste products, fashion designing, beauty treatment, and so on.

On the other hand, the adults of the older age group may have the opinion that it is difficult for them to come to 'Pragati Centre' which may be because of their illness which may not be so for the younger age group as the older people may fall sick frequently and they may get tired soon.

Educational Level

The adults who have low education may give the opinion that Adult Education Programme increased their knowledge and literacy level. Or they may think that they are getting an opportunity to come to college even if it is for three months only as the people with low level of education may be always looking for an opportunity to increase the level of literacy.

The adults, on the other hand who have a medium level of education, may opine that the Adult Education Programme helps in developing an ambition in life as the adults develop an aim in their life before finishing the secondary school.

Similarly, the adults with high level of education may have opinions that it is interesting to learn new recipes and they may have better suggestions regarding the effectiveness of adult education programme as they may have more experience.

Regularity in Attendance

The adults who regularly attend the adult education classes may be highly interested in knowing 'what next', i.e., what activity is going to be conducted in the next class and what issue is going to be discussed. As regularity generates interest so those who are interested in the Adult Education Programme may have many opinions and suggestions regarding the betterment of the programme. The adults who are irregular because of some reason may not have many ideas regarding the manner in which the adult education classes are conducted so they may not opine positively regarding the Adult Education Programme.

The adults who are irregular may not have many friends in the Adult Education Programme with whom they can come to attend the class, share and discuss their opinions, knowledge, experiences and ideas. As a result they may feel lonely and may not be able to express their opinion regarding the Adult Education Programme. Those adults who are regular may have many friends in the adult education programme in 'Pragati Centre' with whom the opinions can be shared.

Personality Dimension

There are two faces of a personality of an individual. One is directed towards the outer world and other is directed towards to the inner world. Thus, adults may be either 'extroverts' or 'introverts'.

The adults who are extroverts may be very open to the adult educators. They may have more discussion on the issues covered in the Adult Education Programme in comparison to the adults who are introverts.

Introvert adults may like to work alone, may feel shy to share their ideas, opinions, suggestions, whereas, the adults who are extrovert may have more opinions, suggestions for the Adult Education Programme and may be they are more open in sharing their problems, which affect their regularity in the Adult Education Programme in 'Pragati Centre'.

Motivation to Learn

The adults who have high motivation may have different opinions regarding the Adult Education Programme in comparison to the adults having low motivation. The adults who have high motivation may have more interest in the activities; therefore, they may apply the knowledge which they have gained from the programme, like trying new recipes at home, which they have learnt in class. The adults who have low motivation may have low opinion regarding the curricular aspect, and they may not want any change in the curriculum. They may be satisfied with what is taught in the classes. Those adults who have high motivation may always want to learn something new.

Objectives of the Study

1. To develop the profile of adult learners who attended the Adult Education Programme in 'Pragati Centre' of the Department of Home Science Extension and Communication.
2. To study the overall opinions of the adult learners regarding the Adult Education Programme of 'Pragati Centre' of the Department of-Home Science Extension and Communication in relation to the following aspects.
   a) Curricular aspect
   b) Instructor
   c) Physical aspect
   d) Methods and materials
3. To study the overall differences in the opinions of the adult learners regarding the Adult Education Programme of 'Pragati Centre' of the Department of Extension and Communication in relation to their:
   a) Age
   b) Educational level
   c) Regularity in attendance
   d) Personality Dimension
   e) Motivation to learn
4. To find out the reasons given by the adult learners for not attending the Adult Education Programme of 'Pragati Centre' of the Department of Home Science Extension and Communication.
5. To obtain suggestions regarding the improvement of the Adult Education Programme of 'Pragati Centre' of the Department Home Science Extension and Communication from the:

a) Adult learners
b) UBS/UCD community volunteers
c) Teacher Supervisors

ASSUMPTIONS OF THE STUDY

1. Adult learners have some opinions regarding the Adult Education Programme of 'Pragati Centre' of the Department of Home Science Extension and Communication.
2. Adult learners have some reasons for not attending the adult education programme of 'Pragati Centre' of the Department of Home Science Extension and Communication.

NULL HYPOTHESES OF THE STUDY

There will be no significant difference in the Adult Education Programme of 'Pragati Centre' of the Department of Home Science Extension and Communication in relation to the following variables:

a) Age
b) Educational level
c) Regularity in attendance
d) Personality Dimension
e) Motivation to learn.

DELIMITATIONS OF THE STUDY

The study is delimited to the Adult Education Programme conducted in 'Pragati Centre' of the Department of Home Science Extension and Communication in the year 2003.

The study is delimited to the adults who have attended the Adult Education Programme in 'Pragati Centre' of the Department of Home Science Extension and Communication.

2

Adult Education: National and International

The present investigation is a study of "An appraisal of adult. education programme of 'Pragati Centre' of the Department of Home Science Extension and Communication, Faculty of Home Science, The M.S. University, Baroda, Gujarat in the year 2003-2004. Extensive perusal of related literature was done in order to comprehend the prior work done in the area of adult education. The investigator had visited Women Studies and research Centre (WSRC), Smt. Hansa Mehta Library, Centre for Advance Studies in Education (CASE) and the library of Department of Home Science Extension and Communication, Faculty of Home Science, The M.S. University of Baroda, Gujarat.

This chapter of related literature is presented under two sections:

1. Studies conducted abroad
2. Studies conducted in India

Studies Conducted Abroad

Omoruyi (2001) conducted a study on the dilemma of women in adult literacy education programme in Benin Metropolis. The objectives of the study were to find out the forces of dilemma and to ascertain whether the delivery structure of the programme was satisfactory. The sample for the study consisted of 60 women participants. The findings revealed that the respondents agreed that social stigma, emotional problems, marital problems, psychological problems, location, discrepancy between content and need, poor learning environment and duration of programme as the contending forces including the dilemma of women in adult literacy programme in the area. The findings of the study were also indicative of the fact that the quality of the programme and provision of instructional aids are unsatisfactory. It was interesting to find that timing, duration of classes, pattern of teaching and instructor-learners relationship were satisfactory.

Kweka (1994) conducted a study on adult education for self-reliance in community health education programme in Tanzania. The objectives of the programme were to provide training in health, sanitation and water, and to create self-reliance in community health education at the grassroots level.

The findings revealed that 47 per cent of the groups were able to manage to construct a rock well; 58 per cent of all the groups were able to cultivate the vegetable gardens, 76 per cent of the groups were able to construct the latrines. There was significant increase in the knowledge related to health and sanitation of about 50 per cent as a result of attending the adult education meetings.

Youssef et al (1992) evaluated the non-formal education programme in Morocco. The major objective of this study were to prepare the Moroccan women to be a responsible and productive citizen who were aware of their familial, social and national responsibility and to provide a productive means of occupying the time of female public school dropouts. The Foyers Feminist programme involved about 45,000 girls in 336 centres nation wide. One hundred and eight centres were located in urban areas and 208 in rural areas. It was found that literacy component of these programmes is either weak or non-existent. It was also found that very few centres provided training in employment to the adolescents. It was further found that the physical structures in which training programmes are housed are inadequate, generally overcrowded with poor sanitary and lighting facilities. The equipments were minimal and teachers were poorly paid and poorly trained.

Chomsri (1989) conducted a study on non-formal education in Thailand. The major objective of this study was to find efficiency of the non-formal education programme. A survey was conducted to identify those who did not complete grade four or primary education and are unable to read and write simple Thai language. The findings revealed that the older people are unwilling to get education from younger people. It was also found that very raw hands without any basic qualification and training in the field of education are recruited to impart education. There was one positive finding that those who had completed a functional literacy course were remarkably articulate and able to express their views in local meetings and also these people were found, actively indulging in the village development programme and planning.

Chomcheum (1984) conducted a study of non-formal vocational education programme in the educational region of Thailand. The major objectives were to study the various organisational and administrative aspects of the non-formal vocational education programme and to study the academic aspects of the programmme. The sample included 15 administrators, 60 instructors and 750 learners. A Questionnaire, a checklist, observations and interview schedule were used for data collection. The findings of the organisational aspect of the programme revealed that administrators were experienced in teaching for about seven years, fifty per cent of the instructors had completed primary and secondary education, all administrators specified that orientation/training programme were necessary but the budget was not sufficient to conduct the adult education classes. The findings of the academic aspect of the programme revealed that 67 per cent of administrators and instructors stated that available courses were sufficient for the learners, the instructors used seminar-cum-workshop, lecture-cum-demonstration for teaching. The evaluation procedure was during and after each instructional period and after completing each unit.

Nunn (1976) conducted a study on an analysis of characteristics and attitude of participants in short-term continuing education classes in an urban situation in USA. The purpose of the study was to identify selected significant characteristics and attitudes of participants in short term continuing education classes. A random stratified and proportional sample composed of 213 persons attending 25 classes responded to a 4-4 items questionnaire. The questionnaire was also designed to get general information concerning the socio-economic status and continuing education, characteristics of participants and their preference, educational plans, interests in subject areas and reasons for enrolment. The findings of the study were: A majority of the respondents were women, under 35 years of age, married and employed full tine in a white collar-job. A majority were first time participants in continuing education classes and desired formal recognition for participation. A majority enrolled for the personal satisfaction reasons as opposed to the job-related reasons and planned a definite or possible enrolment in order to continue personal growth or because participation was rewarding and satisfying. Nearly half of the respondents felt that the largest desirable class should not exceed 25 persons. Respondents most frequently expressed preferences for institutional services related to the desirability of an educational newsletter and the use of counseling services.

Moody (1976) conducted a study at the University of Pacific, USA, on the effectiveness of contacting non-attending adult students as measured by return attendance dropouts and reenrolment The purposes of the study were to analyses (1) the proportion of classes students attended after being absent and then being contacted by a volunteer (2) The dropout rata of students after being contacted by a volunteer and (3) the enrolment rata of students after being contacted by a volunteer. The sample for this study was 53 man and 149 women within and outside of Sacramento and the respondents were randomly assigned to one of four contact methods, i.e., personal, telephone, letter or no contact. Volunteer high school students were the contractors. The findings of the study were as follows: Students returned during the first three weeks period in significantly higher proportions than during the second three weeks period. Students dropped out less after being contacted during tri-first week than during tri-second week. Women dropped out of adult school in higher proportion than men. Men returned to class insignificantly higher proportion than women after being contacted. The highest return attendance rate of students were at 9.00 a.m. and the lowest return attendance rate was at 8.00 a.m. and 8.00 p.m.

Mellon (1974) conducted a study on a comparison of characteristics and factors of adult education participants enrolled in two selected schools in OkLahama City, USA. The purposes of the study were to determine whether adult education students in two different schools were similar or different reasons enrol in adult education programme and whether there is a statistically significant difference between the number of personal reasons indicated by participants enrolled in selected adult education centers, according to their social characteristics and degree of social commitment. Students from high average income areas were attending one school, while students from low average income area were attending the other school. Findings of the study were as follows: Adult students in the two schools did not differ significantly in most of the characteristics which were studied. The students attended the classes regardless of the fact whether they were conducted in high or low income areas. Adult students in both the schools enrolled in adult education classes because of some reasons as they wanted to increase their knowledge and qualify for better paying jobs. The students travelled 14 miles or more to attend the adult education classes if the programme was designed to meet their felt needs.

Miller (1975) carried out an investigation which was concerned with the conditions under which the audio-visual teaching carrel (AVTC) was feasible to instruction method used by Co-operative Extension in New York State. It was found that the adoption of audiovisual teaching carrel did improve the efficiency of disseminating information, since extension programme was able to reach more persons in shorter period of time. Persons under 21 years and those with lower level of education were found to be more satisfied with the carrel than the adults users and the persons with high level of education.

Perdiue (1967) conducted a study on the reasons for participation of a select group of low Income women in sewing classes in Illinois. The purpose of this study was to determine the motivation of a select group of low income families sponsored by the Office of Economic Opportunity. They included an equal number of Negro and Caucasian women, "Sixty per cent of the women attended every class to learn to sew in order to save money. Seventy-six per cent of the women preferred to sew themselves. Only forty-eight per cent of the women wanted to make clothing for other members of their family".

Srinilta (1967) conducted a study on the reasons for participation in women and youth groups in two development areas in Thailand. The purpose of the study was to obtain from the members the degree of importance of reasons for joining and remaining in women and youth groups. One hundred and sixty-three members from the north east and south east areas of Thailand responded to the questionnaire. Chi-square was used to test the relationship between the reasons for participation and the variables such as marital status and developmental area, the reasons, "I like to be with others, meeting place is close to my house, and I want to become a better groomed person" were ranked as reasons of great importance. "Many of my friends are participating, so I thought I should follow them. X wanted to have a chance to become a leader of my community, meeting times are convenient for me, and activities provide me with experience needed in my money earnings," were checked as moderately important. The reason, "I wanted to have few hours of being away from the regular duties at home," was ranked as not being important. The reason, "meeting times are convenient for me", was found to be a significantly associated with marital status. The reason, "I want to become a better groomed person" was significant when associated with the develop-mental area.

Another study was conducted by Kjellberg[1] in the year 1968 to study the knowledge gained by women enrolled in adult home-making programmes in Iowa schools. The purpose of the study was to determine the amount of use being made of the information obtained through the adult education classes, and the reasons why adults attended adult home-making classes. Data were obtained from 354 members of 31 Iowa adult home-making classes. Reasons were checked to indicate if they were important as factors influencing attendance. The use of learning and general reaction to the value of the reasons was rated as "much", "some" or "none". Responses indicated that these adults made use of information gained. About half the classes were in the area of clothing and comments indicated that clothing would of continuing interest to adults. The adults indicated that the most influential reasons for their attendance were learning or educational factors, rather than social reasons. "The desire to continue to improve and learn throughout life," was the one most often checked. The majority attended the classes regularly and believed the classes to be of value to them.

Brayan (1962) studied the reasons for dropouts in home demonstration clubs in Gravin County, Oklahoma. The data were collected by personal interviews. The sample consisted of 182 ex-members of home demonstration county whose tenure as a member terminated during the period 1954-1959 inclusive. The main reasons given for dropping-out of the clubs were that the local club was not run well enough to make it interesting and the programme was not interesting or useful.

Chadderdon and Lyle (1955) studied the reasons given by the women of Iowa of United States of America for attending home making classes for adults. They also studied the relationship between the reasons and the following factors: The amount of formal education of the women, the age of the women, the occupation of the husbands of the women, the subject matter area offered for study, the size of the towns in which the classes met.

A questionnaire was given to 1,358 women to collect information during the adult classes. There were 43 reasons in the questionnaire and the women were asked to check the importance of the reasons in columns like 'much', 'some' or 'none' for attendance. The findings of the study were as follows: The following nine reasons were checked as having much importance by 75 per cent or more of the women: I enjoy getting new ideas. I think I ought to keep on learning new things all my life. I wanted to add to my store of knowledge. I wanted to increase my skill. I like the friendly atmosphere in the classes. I enjoy watching a good demonstration. I have always wanted to know more about this subject. I want the satisfaction of getting more education. I like the teacher's way of presenting things.

A general desire to keep on learning seemed to be an important motivating factor for attending the classes as out of the above mentioned nine reasons, four (first, second, thied and eight) were most frequently checked as having much importance. The personality of the teacher, the method of teaching, the conveniency of time and place and the friendly atmosphere of the classes were found to be motivating for attending the classes as a majority of the women checked reasons which were related to these. The following two reasons seemed to be decreased in importance for attendance as the age increased: I have always wanted to know more about this subject, I thought this course might help me to meet the new responsibilities which arise as my family grows. The women of middle age group, that is 36 years to 45 years, differed from the women of other age groups by only one reasons that is, the desire to teach their children things they could learn in class. IT was most commonly checked as having much importance by them than the women from any other age group. The oldest women were least concerned about the reasons regarding meeting new family responsibilities, learning about the particular subject or adding to their store of knowledge.

Bwatava (1975) investigated a programme of adult education for the national programme charged with reduction of illiteracy in Tanzania. The questionnaires were mailed to all seventeen Regional educational officers in Tanzania who were involved in the administration of adult education. The findings indicated the need to improve the teaching system in terms of transportation, pay and teaching materials. The review of the research studies revealed the following outstanding facts: Very few studies have been done regarding the problems of the teachers and the organisers. A majority of the studies have been done by using the questionnaire The problems faced were regarding lack of teaching materials, audiovisual aids, space, motivation and participation by the adults.

In the year 1975 Cheng Sun conducted a study on the orientations towards non-participation in adult education in USA. The purposes of this study were (1) to identify clusters of reasons to which adults respond similarly when questioned about their saliency to non-participation in educational activities. (2) To assess the reported levels of influence of each cluster of reasons for each individual adult. (3) To relate these levels systematically to individual characteristics and (4) To relate then: to the extent participation among the same groups of adults. The respondents were selected from those people who were not taking part in educational activities at the time they responded to the instrument. The sample was composed of 278 respondents who were working in different types of business concerns. A questionnaire regarding the reasons for non-participation was prepared to assess the reported levels of influence of each cluster of reasons. The leisure activity survey was also completed by each respondents as a measure of the extent of his educational participation and demographic data.

The findings of the study were as follows: The reasons which prevent adults from participating in adult education classes can be categorised into nine clusters such as. Not enough time, Too difficult to succeed, Against the social norms, Too difficult to participate, Negative feelings towards institution, Negative prior experiences, Results not valued, Indifference and unawareness. The clusters scores also showed variations in some demographic characteristics, especially in formal education attainment. 'Not enough time' and 'indifference' were the most influential reasons among the nine clusters. 'Against the social norms' and 'unawareness' were the two influential reasons for participating in adult education classes and 'negative prior experiences' and 'too difficult to succeed' were the two influential reasons for not participating in adult education classes.

Studies Conducted in India

Dangi et al (2002) conducted a study with the major objective to study the different personal and institutional factors, which were responsible for motivating the adults of Dungarpur to join total literacy campaign. All the villagers of Dungarpur district falling within the radius of 2-20 km from the panchayat samiti headquarters were arranged in a descending order on the basis of their population. Then two villages from each cluster were picked up for the study. Ten male and ten female beneficiaries were drawn from each of the six selected villages. Thus, the total sample size of respondents add up to 120 (60 males and 60 females). An interview schedule was used and a face-to-face contact was done for data collection. The study was based on the 'ex-post-facto' research design. The findings revealed that the most important motivational factors responsible for participation of adults in successful completion of TLC were:

- to be able to read and write
- to be able to sign
- the timing of the centre was suitable
- centre was near their house.

The personal and institutional motivating factors were similar among male and female adults.

Das et al (2002) conducted a study on the impact of literacy campaign on health, hygiene, conservation of environment and national integration in Pragjyotishpur of Assam. The major objective of this study was to evaluate the impact of literacy campaign on health, hygiene, conservation of environment and awareness towards national integration of the people of Pragjyotishpur. In this study nine villages were randomly selected in Pragjyotishpur of Kamrup district, covering a total of 90 households of 10 samples in each village. The data were collected with the help of questionnaires and personal interview method. The findings revealed that there was a change in life-style of all the learners and volunteer instructors about health and hygiene status. There was awareness towards conservation of environment by all the respondents. It was also found that participation in the national integration programme indicates the positive sign of development of the respondents.

Surapa (2002) conducted a study on an evaluation of Akshara Sankranthi Programme. The main objective of the evaluation was to assess the percentage of targets and learning skills achieved by the learners. Nine mandals were selected for this study. Four mandals from Vizianagaram and five mandals from Parvathipuram division of Andhra Pradesh were selected for this study. Altogether 450 learners from 45 villages have gone through the examination. The findings revealed that out of total 450 learners only 99 were qualified according to NLM norm. Out of 99 qualified learners, 63 learners were from Vizianagaram division and the rest of them belonged to Parvathipuram division. It was also found that younger age groups and those who had household duties showed much interest by attending classes regularly and their level of achievement was much more in comparison to others who were irregular in attending the classes.

Bhatia and Kumar (2001) conducted a study on neo-literates of Delhi Sarv Shiksha Abhiyan. The major objective of this study was to study the process of becoming literate and to study the learning needs of neo-literates. Twenty cases were studied in-depth. Out of these 10 were selected from those who had passed basic literacy but not participated in post-literacy. The method for data collection for case study was personal interview, observation and information through key informants and six volunteer instructors were interviewed with the help of an interview schedule. The findings revealed that a majority of the respondents had not had primary education due to extreme poverty. A majority of the respondents had problems in their daily life. The major problems included difficult situations arising as a result of their inability to read bus number, transaction of money, etc. These reasons formed a major impetus to join the literacy classes. A reason for dropping out of literacy classes was unavailability of time. The single need, which was emphasized by one and all, was need for vocational or job related training.

Sharma (2000) conducted a comparative study of attitudes of rural and urban adult learners towards literacy campaigns. The major objectives of this study were to find out differences in attitude, learner's awareness on issues discussed in the literacy classes and the attitude of different community members towards literacy campaign. The sample consisted of 200 rural and 165 urban adult learners from five urban and five rural area of Mohali subdivision of Ropar district. A questionnaire was used for collecting the data. The findings revealed that rural learners had a more favourable attitude towards the concept of total literacy campaign as compared to urban. It was also found that more urban as compared to rural learners were aware of the issues which were discussed in the literacy classes.

Gupta (1986) conducted a comparative study of three visual aids in imparting non-formal education to urban adolescent girls and women belonging to the three welfare centres of Baroda. The major objective of this study was to find out the impact of three visual aids (flash cards, puppet and slides) in improving the knowledge and in changing the opinion through the non-formal education of urban adolescent girls and young women belonging to the two selected labour welfare centres of Baroda. The sample consisted of 75 adolescent girls and women. A questionnaire cum checklist was prepared for data collection. The findings revealed that significant difference were found in the gain score showing the overall impact and overall change in opinion regarding educating girls and women and supplementary income activities, through flashcards, puppet and slides. It was found that gain score of flashcards were higher than puppets and slides.

Thakur (1986) conducted a study on problems and job satisfaction of adult literacy teachers of Dabhoi Taluka. The major objective of this study was to find out the problems and job satisfaction of adult literacy teachers of Dabhoi taluka of Baroda district. The sample consisted of 75 adult teachers of Dabhoi Taluka. An interview schedule was used to collect the data.

Findings revealed that teachers faced problems in motivating the learners by organising general meetings as well as by meeting individually. They also faced problems in teaching and evaluating the adult learner because of their irregularity. They found difficulties in conducting the classes at night. It was also found that adult literacy teachers were not satisfied with the salary but they were satisfied with their job because they had complete freedom to conduct the classes.

Shukla (1985) conducted a study on the effectiveness of communication strategies through demonstration and workshop in non-formal education centres. The major objective of this study was to study the effectiveness of communication among adult educators and women through demonstrations and workshops in non-formal education centre' Pragati.' Thirty-seven women were selected for this study who attended the non-formal education classes during the year 1984-85 in the Department of Home Science Extension and Communication, Faculty of Home Science, the M.S. University, Baroda. A questionnaire was used for data collection. Findings revealed that demonstration was found to be more effective method than workshop method. Majority of the women completely agreed with the effectiveness of different aspects of the demonstration.

Ganguli et al (1985) conducted a study on an appraisal of adult education programme in Bihar. The major objective of this study was to evaluate the adult education programme implemented through the state government in the Dumka district of Bihar. The sample consisted of 290 adult learners from 58 centres of Bihar. Interview schedule was used for data collection. The findings of the study revealed that the learners joined the programme basically to acquire the skills of reading and writing and the main source of motivation in both the projects was the instructor. But learners were not sure of the utility of the programme. The main reason for the dropouts was that family problems came in the way of learning. Further, it was found that as compared to reading and writing ability, the achievement of the learners in numeracy appeared to be poor.

Pathak (1984) conducted a study to find out the effectiveness of puppetry as a method for educating rural adult women. The study was aimed to find out the effectiveness of puppetry, in acquiring knowledge and changing opinions regarding parent education, health and social evils and to find out the relation of age, education, religion and family income in acquiring knowledge and changing opinions. A group of 50 women comprised the sample of the study. These were the women who were pretested, who had attended all the puppet plays and whose pretest score was less than 80 per cent. Pretest and post-test were administered to find out the effectiveness of puppetry in acquiring knowledge and changing opinions. The major conclusion of the study were: The overall and topic-wise change in opinions of rural women as a result of using puppetry as a method of education was significant. Women belonging to each category of age, education, religion and family income showed significant change in opinions in all the subject matter areas. Change in opinions was retained best in the area of social evils. It was also found that better retention of change in opinions was shown by older adults, the group with low education and the group with low income.

Kanitkar (1983) studied the impact of puppets in different parts of India. The objectives of the several experiments conducted were to organise a local puppet troup depicting themes based on their concerns, to judge the impact of the puppetry performance on the viewing audience and to create awareness and stimulate action. The performances carried out in two villages, Labhoyachi Vadi of Raigad district in Maharashtra and Van Kusawada on the hill top of Koyana dam, both with a majority of illiterate tribal population, led to the following conclusion: Puppets can make an impact, if properly used with the active participation of local people and in local dialect. Besides being low cost, easy to adopt and handle and very much Indian in nature, puppetry as a medium attracts all age groups. On the basis of the case studies the investigator suggests that the role of a communicator should never be fixed, only to communicate. He should gather information about the community and people in all related areas of life and try to interpret. The investigator felt that there may be many more plus points in this medium but it cannot be claimed as a complete medium of people's communication. Its effective use lied in working out suitable combination with inter-personal and group dialogue.

Bhatnagar (1982) conducted a study with the purpose of knowing the effectiveness of some of the modern and traditional audiovisual aids. It was an experiment with pretest-posttest design. Ten villages were selected randomly from two purposively selected panchayat samitis of Udaipur district of Rajasthan. For each village a group of 20 to 25 farm women were selected randomly to whom a knowledge test was administered. On the basis of scores obtained, a homogeneous group of 15 farm women were selected from each village forming a sample of 150 farm women. The following aids were selected: the modern radio, the traditional puppet and *kavad,* projected slides and non-projected flipbook. Only one audiovisual aid was exposed in each pair of the 10 selected villages. Drying of vegetables was the subject matter for communication. The knowledge test was administered three times as pretest, posttest and retention test. The aids were compared for their effectiveness in terms of gain and retention of knowledge and were ranked on the basis of a Relative Efficiency Index.

Bastia (1981) conducted a study on National Adult Education Programme in tribal region of Orissa state. The major objective was to study the implementation of the national adult education programme in the tribal region of Orissa state. The sample consisted of 40 adult education centres in which 40 instructors, 306 learners, 58 dropouts, 108 illiterate adults, 107 community leaders were selected for this study interview, observation schedule and achievement test were used for data collection. The findings revealed that large majority of the centres had no proper lighting facilities, inadequate seating arrangement and unsatisfactory sanitary facilities. The reasons mentioned for dropping out were inconvenient location and timing of centres, irrelevance of curriculum and rigid behaviour of instructors. It was also found that the different tribal communities use various types of tribal languages, it had become very difficult to prepare materials in these languages.

Natarajan (1981) conducted a critical study to evaluate the performance of the National Adult Education Programme at Amarpur block in Bhagalpur district, Bihar. The data were collected by interviewing the adult literacy teachers. The investigator collected information regarding (1) the adequacy of physical facilities, (2) irregular attendance of learners, (3) model of enrolment of learner in adult literacy centres. The major findings of the study as follows: Adult literacy teachers were not satisfied with the sitting arrangement in the class. Sufficient number of books was not provided. Twenty-two per cent adult learners regularly attend the adult literacy class; 83.9 per cent of adult literacy teachers enrolled learners' names by door to door approach; 12.9 per cent of adult literacy teachers enrolled learners' names with the cooperation of village leaders. In this study adult literacy teachers were asked to list suggestions which could improve the overall quality of the programme. A few suggestions given by them were as follows: The venue of the adult literacy centre should be proper. The different communities should be adequately represented in the centre. Good and comfortable setting arrangement should be made. Reading material should be supplied in time.

B. Kaur (1981) conducted a critical study to find out the problems of adult literacy teachers of Baroda district. The purposes of the study were to identify the adult literacy teacher's problems in the areas of motivation, physical facili-ties, teaching aids and evaluation methods. The major findings of the study were as follows: The adult literacy teachers faced problems in motivation. Location of the adult literacy centres was not suitable. Adequate number of teaching aids were not supplied on time. Less number of attendances made it difficult in evaluation.

Sharma and Sharma (1981) investigated into the problems of adult literacy teachers of New Delhi. The purposes of the study were: to identify the problems recognised by adult literacy teachers with regards to motivation, teaching method, physical facilities and teaching aids. The data were collected by a questionnaire. The major findings were as follows: Location of adult literacy centre unsuitable. Supply of reading material irregular. Visual aids not provided. Fan not available. Kerosene on difficult to get. Desks not supplied for learners and mats inadequate. Reluctant learners who did not want to attend classes.

Barthakur (1980) conducted a study to find out the problems faced by Mukhya sevikas in implementing the Applied Nutrition Programmes in Gujarat. The objectives of the study were to find out the problem dominated areas; intensity of problems; problems in different schemes of applied nutrition programmes and significant association between the problems and background characteristics of the respondents: years of experience, training, language ability and qualifications. The population of the study consisted of all the Mukhya sevikas of Applied Nutrition Programme blocks of different districts of Gujarat during the fifth five year plan covering totally 89 blocks of the state, closed end questionnaire was mailed to the respondents for collecting the data. The major findings of the study were as follows: Mukhya sevikas faced the problem of non-participation and non-cooperation of the villagers in the programme. There were inadequate supplies and services and poor housing and communication facilities. They also faced the organisational problems which were mainly of inadequacy of training, lack of interest and initiative taken by the superior officers. A significant association was found between the respondents facing problems and their years of experience only.

Patel (1979) undertook a study to construct a tool for measuring the attitude of the teacher-educators towards the programmes of non-formal education leading to lifelong education. An attitude scale on the Likert type technique was developed. Some of the findings revealed that the attitudes of teacher educators of the urban areas were more favourable towards the components of need and importance of non-formal education programmes than those of semi-urban areas. Teacher educators of South Gujarat region, had a more favourable attitude than those of Central Gujarat. Older teachers had a more favourable attitude than the middle-aged teachers. Female teachers had a slightly more favourable attitude than the male teacher educators.

Patel (1978) conducted a study of Activities of three Labour Welfare Centres in Baroda city and women participation. One of the main objectives of the study was to find out the general attitude of women participants towards the activities of the center. Through purposeful random sampling 40 participants were interviewed, and the findings revealed that: As age increased there was decrease in the favourableness of the attitudes towards the activities. Young adolescent participants, who had primary and secondary education, had a more favourable attitude compared to the ones who had either less or no education at all. With the increase in the income level there was increase in the unfavourableness of attitude. The Department of Adult and Continuing Education, University of Madras, (1979) undertook a sample study of learner's attitude in nine adult education centres, in Madras. An interview schedule, with eight questions, to elicit information concerning their concept of education, causes for dropping out, in addition to their biographic data was collected from 150 rural adults who attended the classes.

Bishnoi (1978) conducted a study to find out the reasons given by the adult women for not attending the adult education classes in sewing in the Labour Welfare Centres with respect to their socio-economic status, age and education. It had an aim to find out the homemaking interests of the women. The sample consisted of the hundred women, residing in Akota, Fatehpura and Gorwa communities of Baroda where the Labour Welfare Centres are situated. The women were selected in such a way that there were almost equal number of women in the socio-economic status groups, education level groups and age groups from the same hundred women. All the hundred women were married and 80 per cent of the women were from nuclear families. Ninty-five per cent of the women were not employed outside the home gainfully. Only 8 per cent of the women had more than one female member of 18 years of age besides themselves in their families. Little less than half of the women had the children in each of this age groups: four years to six years, seven years to nine years and above twelve years. Sixty per cent of the respondents had five to seven members in their families. Two per cent of the respondents from the low socio-economic status group had more than eleven members in their families, while none of the respondents from the high socio-economic status group had these many members in their families. The area 'Time' was the only area, in which the four reasons cut of the total 10 reasons were reported by more than 50 per cent of the respondents for absence from the classes, while in the rest of the areas the highest percentages of the respondents reporting the reasons for not attending the classes were less than 50 per cent. A majority of the reasons in the areas of 'teacher', 'place' and social status, religion and social belief were reported by less than one-tenth of the respondents for not attending the classes.

Shah (1978) conducted a critical study of the programmes of non-formal education in Baroda city and their impact on the community. The case studies of such eight agencies showed the following hindering factors in the progress of the programme: Audio visual aids of good quality were not in sufficient number. Space was inadequate at the place where classes were conducted. In the beginning the motivation for literacy education among the women was lacking. Their main fear was that it will not be possible to learn at an advanced stage. Adults had difficulty in bringing their own material as they were from extremely poor families. Community people and the family members criticised the programmes for women and tried to discourage them. Household difficulties came in the way of attending the classes regularly. There was lack of motivation on the part of learners as it was felt that it is extremely difficult to motivate the people for the non-formal education programmes. It became difficult to sell the garments made by women due to lack and differentiation in skills.

N. Ventakaiah (1977), while studying the impact of the farmer's Functional Literacy Programme on the participants in Andhra Pradesh, considered attitudinal change towards improvement of agricultural practices and adult literacy as one of the form of assessment of impact. For this, an attitude scale on adult literacy was developed. This study was experimental in nature and, through stratified random sampling technique, a sample of 540 adults participating in farmer's functional literacy were selected for the experimental group, while, 240 adult literate farmers not participating and not belonging to the experimental village were selected for the control group. Some of the major findings of the study showed that the experimental group had significantly higher knowledge in modern agriculture practices and a more favourable attitude towards improved agricultural practices and adult literacy than their counterparts in the control group. A significant impact of the programme in respect of attitudes towards modern agricultural practices and adult literacy was also found in all the age groups, caste groups, land holding groups and, socio-economic status categories of the participants. Attempts to study attitudes of adults towards Adult Continuing Education were made by Botsman (1975), Orme (1975) and Vanover (1977) in different states of USA. In all the three cases a questionnaire was administered by the investigators. Though the respondents in all the three studies included both male and female adults it was found that females constituted the majority. The findings revealed that most of the adults had a favourable attitude towards adult continuing education and, they expressed the desire to continue learning. Younger adults were more interested in learning that the older ones. The main reasons for enrolment were to gain personal and social satisfaction.

Gayatonde (1977) studied the problems of social education in India with special reference to Maharashtra, Gujarat, Rajasthan, Madhya Pradesh and Karnataka. One of the objectives of the study was to appraise the attitudes of the Intellectual elite regarding social education. The tool employed was a Likert type attitude scale constructed in the regional language of the states from where a total sample of 362 respondents was selected. The "deeply interested" people from the sample were later on interviewed. Some of the major findings revealed that though social education officers felt that social change would be affected by social education, intellectuals did not think that social education was an effective agent of social change. It was also felt that, the content of social education should be based on criteria like, development of the potential of the adult, creation and development of interest, assistance to the individual in problem solving and, so on.

Gupta (1975) conducted a study on differences in leisure time interests of the suburban home makers according to the selected variables age of the housewife, family income, education of the housewife, type of the family and size of the family. A check-sheet was used as a tool for the collection of data on leisure time interests. The population of the study consisted of 120 suburban homemaker of three selected housing colonies of Baroda. The findings of the study were: A majority of home makers from all the three colonies belonged to single families. A majority of home-makers were found to be in young age group and middle age group and they also belonged to small and middle families. All the home-makers were from middle income group and high income group. Mostly ladies had leisure time in the afternoon and evening. A majority of home makers were found to be in educated and highly educated group. The home-makers were ready to spend an average sum of Rs.13/- per month to meet their leisure time interests. All the home-makers were highly interested in recreational and social activities. The respondents from joint families were more interested in recreational and social activities.

The respondents of young age were more interested in physical activities when compared with those of middle age and old age home makers. The home-makers belonging to middle age group were found to be more interested in educational activities. The respondents from small families revealed higher interests for physical, creative, social, educational and recreational activities whereas middle sized families were found to be highly interested in religious and other activities. The respondents from educated and highly educated group were found to be interested in social activities and other activities, for example, attending public speeches, trying out new recipes, etc. The respondents from high income group were found to be more interested in all the activities, for example, recreational activities, social, religious and other activities, education and physical activities as they could spend more to meet their leisure time interests.

Talukdar (1975) studied adult education in Assam during post-independence period. The purpose of the present study was to study whether education is maintaining the status quo or it has been able to progress in the light of modern day context of adult education. The data were collected through the questionnaire method along with the personal interviews and observations of the literacy work and official visits to some adult education centres. The questionnaires were distributed among the adult people in some selected community development blocks of Assam. The major findings of the study were as follows: Audio-visual aids were not much used in the field of adult education. The organisational problem of adult education was found to be present. Adult education in Assam had received least attention during the first three plan periods. Instructional problems were also found to be present. The factors like dearth of teachers and accomodation, want of suitable time and content of adult education, etc., were found to be standing in the way of progress of adult education. Communication difficulty was found to be another handicap.

Bandari (1974) tried to study the factors which affected retention and, dropout in adult literacy classes in the Udaipur district of Rajasthan state. He found that as far as age was concerned there was no significant difference between the persistent and dropouts. Significant differences with respect to the content of learning existed between participants of literacy and functional literacy classes. The reasons given the dropouts were day work, domestic work, ridicule by friends and relatives. Factors in persistence were, need to write letters and to sign, read religious books, maintain records and accounts, to learn the language and to utilise leisure time constructively.

Sinha (1973) conducted a study to evaluate the performance of the National Adult Education Programme at Jamar Block in Bihar. Data were collected by interviewing adult literacy teachers. The investigator collected information regarding (1) attendance of the learner, (2) physical facilities. The major findings of the study were as follows: Average attendance at female centres is significantly smaller than male centers. Sufficient number of teaching aids was not supplied. Poor lighting facilities disturbed in teaching. Adult literacy teachers were not satisfied with sitting arrangement in the class. Some of the adult literacy teachers were asked to list suggestions which could improve the overall quality of the programme administered in the centre. The choice of the location of adult literacy centers should be made on survey data. Center should not be open in haste. Adult literacy centres having insufficient attendance should be merged. Seating arrangements at the centres should be improved. The different developmental government departments should be involved in the programme. The adult literacy teachers need more training for discharging their duties meaningfully.

Wiesinqer (1973), while discussing about WOAL—Work Oriented Adult Literacy programme for women—wrote that the traditional primer used for teaching alphabets was discarded and it was replaced by a daily session sheet. Posters, flashcards, flannel boards, speedometers and new sheets were used as supporting materials. Regarding methods, a completely unconventional approach was tried. The new approach of teaching functional literacy consisted of the following five steps sequence per week: 'Discussion - Demonstration -Practice - Literacy teaching – Assimilation'.

Chandra (1972) conducted a study on adult education in home-making. The purposes of this study were to investigate the extent of acceptance of adult education in home-making and to discover the relationship of age, income and educational level of women to their acceptance of home-making education. There were three selected programmes, namely, food demonstration, clothing construction workshop and decorative art workshop in home-making education. The data were collected from a random sample of 327 urban home-makers of the seven selected communities of Baroda. The findings of the study were as follows: The largest percentages of all the groups of home-makers indicated high acceptance of food demonstrations. The second in preference for the youngest and the younger home-makers was the clothing construction workshops, whereas, for the young home-makers it was decorative arts. The age of the urban home makers significantly affected the acceptance of all the three types of adult home-making programmes. The younger the age the higher was the acceptance of adult programmes. Education produced a significant effect on the acceptance of only adult programmes of clothing construction and decorative arts. The higher the education, the higher was the acceptance of adult programmes. The family income of the urban home-makers was significantly related to all the three types of adult programmes. Higher income was associated with low acceptance of adult programmes in foods and clothing construction. Decorative arts were rejected by almost one half of the home-makers, having low, middle or high incomes.

Hazarika (1971) studied the reasons given by the women for not attending the adult education classes conducted by the undergraduate students of the Home Science Education and Extension Department of the Faculty of Home Science, Baroda. The frequency of the reasons with respect to their socio-economic status and the age of the women was also studied. A questionnaire was used to collect the data and the sample of different age and socio-economic status groups was selected from the seven communities of Baroda in which the classes were conducted during the years 1967 to 1970. The findings of the study were as follows: On an average no reason in any of the areas of reasons except "time" was responsible for keeping the women of any socio-economic status or age groups absent either, most of the times or very often from the adult education classes. Most of the women did not attend the adult education classes in Home Science most of the times for the lack of time as they had household work, had to look after the young children. Sometimes they did not attend the adult education classes in Home Science because of: frequent guests, return of husband and children from the office and school respectively during the class period. The women from the young age group did not attend the adult education classes because they: already knew some of the things taught in the classes, had household work, were not interested in the class activities. The women from the middle age group, besides the above two reasons, had one more reason: that they were suffering from several minor illnesses. The women from the old-2age group, besides the last two reasons had the two more reasons that they did not know the exact time of the classes and were not physically well. The women from the upper socio-economic status did not attend the classes because they were not interested in the class activities, already knew some of the things taught in the classes, did not know the exact time of the classes, did not know the meeting place, did not know the type of work taught in the classes. The women from the upper middle socio-economic status, besides these reasons, had one more reason: that they used to get their clothes stitched by the tailor. The women from lower middle socio-economic status, besides the above reasons, had one more reason: that they were not physically well. The higher the socio-economic status, the greater was the number of the women having the higher frequency of the reasons for not attending the adult education classes in the area of time and publicity. The older the women, the greater was the number of the women having the higher frequency of the reasons for not attending the adult education classes in Home Science in the area of health.

Shrivastava (1970) investigated the educational problems of the Lanjia Saora areas of Orissa, a tribal educational unit. The purpose of the study was to identify the educational problems of Langia Saora areas of Orissa, tribal educational unit under three major dimensions: (1) educational administration, (2) wastage and failure, (3) socio-economic problems effecting education. The major findings of the study were as follows: The progress of education was hindered by administrative problems such as lack of social building, management, trained teachers, teaching materials and proper inspection of the schools. Teachers needed to be given better facilities to work more effectively. The supply of reading and writing materials to the students were unsatisfactory. Attendance in the adult classes was very poor.

Lack of motivation among the adults was one of the major problems.

Sharma (1970) conducted a study to find out the difficulties faced by the teachers of adult literacy classes of Patiala district of Punjab. The purpose of the study was to find out the problems of adult literacy teachers in the areas of motivation, physical facilities and teaching aids. The major findings of this study were as follows: No suitable places for running the adult literacy classes. Irregular attendance of adult learners. Lack of interest of the villagers in the adult literacy scheme. Paucity of teaching aids. Reading materials were unsuitable and inadequate.

Patel (1970) did a critical study of Social Education in the state of Gujarat and tried to study public opinion about the present and future programmes of Social Education through an opinionnaire. Respondents differed in their opinions regarding Social Education. For some, it was teaching of 3 R's while, for others in was education for social change. Besides, it was also found that, wastage in Social Education was to a great extent the major deficiency in the programme and 86.6 per cent of women were not attending the classes regularly.

Khurana (1970) conducted a study on the reasons given by the women and the importance of the reasons placed by the women for attending the adult education classes organised and conducted by the under graduate students of the Department of Home Science Education and Extension of the Faculty of Home Science, Baroda. She also studied the relationship between the reasons and the amount of formal education, and the age of the women and occupation of their husbands. A questionnaire was used to collect the data and the sample was selected from three communities of Baroda. The women who have attended a minimum of 50 per cent or more classes during 1968 and 1970 were included. The findings of the study were as follows: Husbands of half of the women were teachers and about one-third were doctors, engineers and lawyers. The women showed a desire to keep on learning and getting new ideas and undertaking creative activities to utilise their leisure time, the method of teaching, the personality of the teacher and the friendly atmosphere of the class. The following reasons were considered to be intensely motivating reasons by 65-per cent and more of the women. Most of these reasons were educational reasons and the women were interested in:

- learning new things,
- watching a good food demonstration,
- getting new ideas.
- knowing what was happening in the classes, increaseing knowledge of Home Science,
- keeping on learning throughout life
- being in a friendly atmosphere of the classes,
- participating in these interesting classes.

The recognition of need for continuing education was evident through the above reasons.

The following reasons were checked by 50 per cent and more of the women in the column 'Never'.

- to keep relation with the supervisor of the classes so that she would help their children in the college,
- to utilise the opportunity to wear new clothes.
- to oblige the supervisor who was their friend. A majority of the women attended the classes voluntarily.
  a) Age was the most influencing factor for the attendance of the women in all the three communities. With advance in age the women were motivated to attend the classes and were interested to continue to learn.
  b) In two communities women with more education were conscious of their needs and aware of utilising their leisure time fruitfully.
  c) The occupation of husband was least influencing factor among all the factors.

A study was conducted in Tamil Nadu for promotion of adult education. Education for all is a basic need and right of every citizen. Illiteracy is a menace to a civilised society, more so in a country of diverse people. Ignorance is exploited by a few ill-intentioned elite for bettering their prospects. The pioneers of the college, sensitive to this problem, as made it a policy and duty to eradicate the intellectual poverty. They had a conviction that education and only education can provide a lasting solution to the problem of material poverty.

Objectives of the practice

- To eradicate slavish mentality and to bring a practice awareness among the rural population about the need for education.

- To prevent dropouts and guide them on the right path; and
- To make the rural students better prepared to pursue higher studies.

Education for all is being implemented at various levels beginning from kindergarten to educated employees. The school dropouts prevention project seeks to prevent children from turning into a street of children, child labourers by offering them intensive assistance to go back to school. Dropout-girls and potential dropout-girls are sponsored by the project to ensure their continued education. They are guided and trained to take up various trades like tailoring, knitting, soap-making etc. All the primary school children of Don Bosco Centre and primary school children from village schools are thoroughly screened by a doctor who is a volunteer on the project. He follows it up with on-the-spot medications, free of charge. The Association of Mathematics Teachers, of the Department of Mathematics, is yet another enterprise in community service catering to the needs of the Mathematics teachers in the schools in and around Tirupattur. Lack of proper inter-connectedness between the college programmes and the village environment and lack of rural orientation in the syllabus are the main obstacles. The autonomous status of the college has helped the faculties to give the syllabus a rural slant. Convincing the parents was an obstacle. Planning programme execution in consultation with the District Education Officer and Headmasters of schools and other local authorities has helped in its smooth implementation. The Total Literacy Drive has made it possible to prevent dropouts; to create environment conducive for studying; to improve the performance in examinations; to empower students to go for higher education; to ensure that the rights of the children are taken care of; and to promote volunteerism and community-based work in the field of education and child empowerment.

Nagappa (1966) and Mullikayunaswamy (1969) took interest in surveying the reading needs and interests of adult neoliterates in Bangalore and Mysore respectively. It was found that religious and folk literature had the highest appeal. Topics related to one's occupation were preferred, familiar topics had a preference over unknown ones. Stories and fiction were the favourite among them. It was concluded that literacy not only stimulated reading hut also widened the scope of reading desires of the adult neoliterates.

Parlikar (1966) studied the past and the present programmes of the Mahila Mandals to determine the relationship between the socio-cultural factors, age, leisure time available to the members, leadership, and the interest and the participation of the Mahila Mandals. The study was conducted in three selected Mahila Mandals in the three selected blocks, namely, Navsari, Chikhli and Bansala in the Bulsar district of the Gujarat state. The interview method combined with the questionnaire was used for collecting data. Part one of the questionnaire included the personal information regarding the members and their families. Part two included the activities which were classified as sewing-man's, woman's and baby's garments, embroidery. Productive art and village crafts. A cheeklist was given to the secretary of the Mahila Mandals to collect information regarding the programme offered and the festivals utilised for carrying out the programme by these Mandals. The questionnaire and the checklist were developed in simple regional language.

The investigator spent four days in each block to collect the data. The findings related to the present study were: all the three Mahila Mandals undertook recreational activities like singing bhajans and educational activities like organising sewing classes, sanitation campaigns and craft classes. Two Mahila Mandals conducted educational activities like learning new recipes and improved farm practices and preparation of compost and sock pits. All the three Mahila Mandals organised fairs and competitions, and utilised all the national festivals. Two Mahila Mandals celebrated religious festivals. About one-third of the members were Brahmin. An equal number, that is, one-fifth of the members were Khatri and backward and scheduled castes. The remaining members were Muslims. Business, farming and service were the main occupations. The family income ranged from below rupees 1,000 to above Rs. 3,600 per year. An equal per cent of members, that is, about 20 per cent were found in the three income groups. They were (a) below Rs. 1,000 (b) between rupees Rs. 1,100 and Rs. 1,500 and (c) above Rs. 3, 600 per year. Half of the members were married, about one-third were unmarried and the remaining were widows. Little more than one-fourth of the members had more than six children while more than one-sixth had no children.

Little more than half of the members had leisure time in the afternoon and about one fifth had at night. The remaining members had either in the morning or in the evening.

About half of the total population attended primary school and about one-tenth no education. Others had either high school education or higher education. The younger members had higher education than the older members.About half of the members' husband had primary school education. Others had either high school educa-tion or no education.

Higher interest was found in making woman's and baby's garments, rangoli, crochet work and duvet-making. None had interest in adult literacy and home nursing classes. When irrespective of the factors, responses were studied, a higher interest was found in activities under sewing, embroidery and productive art than in those under village craft. Brahmin, Khatri and Muslim members, who had higher education than the other castes, showed a higher interest in making woman's and baby's garments. Patidars and other castes who had primary or no education showed interest in making simple garments like *zabla, jangia* and petticoat. A higher interest was found in sewing activities than in activities under productive art and village craft among the members from farm families or who had service. Members from business families showed more interest than other members in activites under productive art and village craft.

In the year 1962, a group of four students from the Faculty of Social Work of Maharaja Sayajirao University of Baroda studied: The people's participation in the programmes conducted by the Labour Welfare Centre, Baroda and the factors responsible for the non-participation of the people. The extent to which the activities of the centre geared to meet the needs of the participants. The group interviewed the personnels of the centre together and make separate notes and compared afterwards.

The group equally distributed the sample of participants and non-participants among themselves for collecting data. Though they prepared separate dissertations, as their objectives, centre, localities and findings were the same. The review of the dissertation of Barge only is presented here. The study was divided into two divisions – (A) Study of the participants. (B) Study of the non-participants. Four localities, namely, GendaFalia,

Harijanvas, KoyaliFalia and Ranavas, were selected for the study by the organisers of the centre as the participation of the people in those areas was low.

The participants and the non-participants were selected by random sampling method. The total number of the male and female participants were 65 and 44 respectively. The group interviewed 50 per cent male and female participants. For non-participants, all from the Harijanvas and 20 per cent from the remaining three localities were taken, persons who were at least 15 years of age were selected for both the participants and the non-participants.

Separate schedules were used to interview the participants and the non-participants, and an interview guide was used to interview the personnels of the centre and the Commissioner of Labour Welfare Board of Ahmedabad. The investigator with the group observed the working of the centre a full day and studied documents to select the participants. The activities of the centre was grouped as (a) Recreational activities, for example, indoor and outdoor games, (b) Educational activities, for example, reading books, newspapers, (c) Vocational activities, for example, sewing, knitting, and (d) Special programmes, for example, celebration of national days. The findings of the study were as follows: A majority of he participants were from the residents just around the centre. A majority of the participants were labourers. Most of the participants had low standard of education and income. Participation of male members was more in recreational and educational programmes and less in special programmes. Participation of female members in vocational activities was satisfactory. The members who participated were interested in these activities as they thought they would help them in their physical and economic development, and they could utilised their leisure time in a productive way.

Rashid (1958) conducted a survey on the non-attendance and drop-outs in the adult literacy classes in certain states of India. According to his non-attendance and dropouts are twin problems faced by adult workers in India as elsewhere. Most failures in the sphere of adult education are attributed to these two factors! The purpose of the study was to find out the reasons why adults dropout. The literacy classes were held in various villages in the states of Karnataka, Gujarat, Punjab, Uttar Pradesh and Delhi. The main aim of the programme was to, "encourage the lower age group of 14 to 35 years to attend the literacy classes. The classes were open to the illiterates and semi-literates. Since there were wide variations in the enrolment there were problems of non-attendance and drop-outs. In one or two cases the school had to be closed down because of low attendance. Some of the reasons for adults dropping out were "migration, change in residence, change in shift of work, sickness - both of individual and family, domestic responsibilities, lack of time and lack of physical and mental ability. From the study it was concluded that the fluctuations between the maximum and minimum enrolment were wide. The study also revealed that April, May and June were the peak months for the adults to earn a better living. During this period they were kept busy till late night which clashed with their school timings; obviously the attendance went down considerably during this period. Among the social factors the most important was the religion of the adult students; for instance, religious festivals led to absence of the students from the classes for several days.

Conclusion

Review of related literature revealed that studies on the adult education programme were conducted in different parts of India as well as abroad. Most of the studies used questionnaire and interview schedule as the method of data collection. The survey method was the common research design. After reviewing the various studies it was found that lack of proper physical facilities was the major problem in conducting the adult education programme. Some of the studies have also found that there was a lack of trained and experienced instructors because of which message delivery was not efficient and effective which led to the failure of the programme and no positive impact was found on the learners. Non-suitability of the timings was also found as a major constraint in conducting the adult education programme. Hence, a study related to these aspects of the adult education programme of 'Pragati centre' was proposed.

3

Descriptive Analysis of Adult Education

The present investigation was aimed at studying "An Appraisal of the Adult Education Programme of 'Pragati Centre' of the Department of Home Science Extension and Communication, Faculty of Home Science, The M.S. University of Baroda in the year 2003-2004." This chapter includes the following aspects:

a) Description of the population
b) Construction of the research tool
c) Validation of the research tool
d) Collection of data
e) Scoring and categorisation
f) Plan of statistical analysis of the data

Description of the Population

The population of the study consisted of the adult learners who attended the Adult Education Programme of 'Pragati Centre' of the Department of Home Science Extension and Communication, Faculty of Home Science in the year 2003. UBS/UCD Community volunteers and teacher supervisors of Adult Education Programme were involved.

The sample consisted of 125 adult learners who attended the Adult Education Programme of 'Pragati Centre' of the Department of Home Science Extension and Communication, Faculty of Home Science in the year 2003, six Urban Basic Services and Urban Community Development Project's Community

Volunteers and four teacher supervisors. The purposive random sampling method was used for selecting the sample.

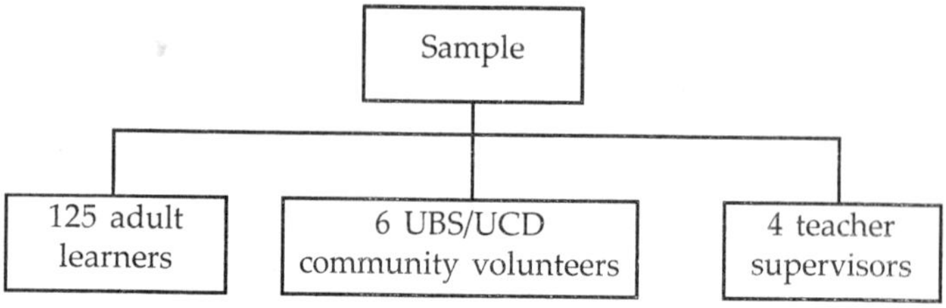

Construction of the Research Tool

A structured questionnaire was developed by the investigator. He constructed the tool after reviewing related literature from journals, articles, reports, books and dissertations.

The questionnaire was divided into four sections.

Section I - Profile of the adult learner

- Background information
- Personality
- Motivation

Section II - Opinions of the adult learners

- Curriculum aspect
- Instructor aspect
- Physical aspect
- Methods and materials aspect

Section III - Reasons for not attending the adult education classes.

Section IV - Suggestions from

- Adult learners
- UBS/UCD Community Volunteers
- Teacher supervisors.

Table 1
Construction of the Tool and the Response System

Sr. No.	*Section*	*Aspects*	*Responsesystem*
1.	Profile of the adult learner	– Age	Checklist
		– Educational level	Checklist
		– Regularity in attondance	Checklist
		– Personality	2-point scale
		– Motivation to learn	4-point scale
2.	Opinions of the adult learners	– Curriculum aspect	3-point scale
		– Instructor	and open
		– Physical aspect	ended.
		– Methods and materials	
3.	Reasons for not attending	–	2-point scale
4.	Suggestions	– Adult learners	
		– UBS/UCD community volunteers	3-point scale and open ended.
		– Teacher Supervisors	

V.S. Shantamani and A. Hafeez's standardised scale, for personality, 1978 (adapted), (JIM) Junior Index of Motivation by Frymier, for motivation to learn, 1988 (adapted).

Validation of the Research Tool

To check the content and construct validity the tool was given to seven different experts. The experts were requested to check.

a) Clarity of ideas,

b) Content validity

c) Appropriateness of instructions

d) Appropriateness of response system

e) Clarity of language.

Out of these, six experts were from the Faculty of Home Science and one expert from the Faculty of Education and Psychology, The M.S.University Baroda, Vadodara.

Changes were made in the questionnaire on the basis of the suggestions and comments received from the experts. The tool was constructed in English and then translated into Gujarati with the help of Gujarati experts for better understanding.

Collection of Data

Data collection was done in the months of December and January 2004. The investigator used home visit method to collect the data from the adult learners and personally contacted UBS/UCD Community volunteers and teacher supervisors in their respective offices.

Scoring and Categorisation

Table

Categorisation of Variables under the Study

Sr. No.	*Variables*	*Basis*	*Category*
1.	Age	– 25 or below 25 years	Young
		– 26 years and above	Old
2.	Educational level	– 8th or below 8th standard	Low
		– 9th to 12th standard	Medium
		– Graduation and above	High
3.	Regularity in attendance	– 15 classes	Regular
		– Less than 15 classes	Irregular
4.	Personality dimension	– 0-10	Introvert
		– 11-20	Extrovert
5.	Motivation to learn	– 0-30	Low motivation
		– 31-60	High motivation

Table 3

Scoring and Categorisation of the Overall Opinions of the Respondents

Scores	*Category*
16-38	Low opinion
39-54	Moderate opinion
55-72	High opinion

Table 4

Categorisation of Other Background Information

Sr.No.	*Background information*	*Basis*	*Category*
1.	Total income of the family (per month)	Rs. 1000-2000 Rs. 2001-4000 Rs. 4001-6000	Low income group Middle income group High income group
2.	Salary of the adult learners (per month)	Rs. 500-1000 Rs. 1001-4000	Low salary High salary
3.	Work experience of the adult learners	Less than one year 1-4 years	Less experience More experience
4.	Working hours of the adult learners	1-4 hours 5-8 hours	Less hours More hours

Item-wise Intensity Indices

Item-wise intensity indices were calculated for all the aspects. The range for indices for the extent of opinions regarding the adult education programme on all the aspects was calculated as follows:

Range	*Extent of Opinions*
1.00 - 1.59	Low
1.60 - 2.59	Moderate
2.60 - 3.00	High

Plan for Statistical Analysis of the Data

Table 5

Statistical measures for the analysis of the data

Sr.No.	*Purpose*	*Statistical measures*
1.	Background information of the respondents	Percentage
2.	Overall opinions reported by the adult learners.	Percentage

(Contd...)

(Contd...)

3.	Overall opinion reported by adult learners according to the variables.	Percentage
4.	Item wise opinions reported by the adult learners.	Intensity Indices
5.	Overall Differences in the opinions according to the variables.	Chi-Square
6.	Reasons for not attending the adult education classes.	Percentage
7.	Suggestions from the-	
	– Adult learners	Percentage
	– UBS/UCD Community Volunteers	Percentage
	– Teacher supervisors.	Percentage

4

Adult Education: Methods and Practices

This chapter presents the findings of investigation of "An appraisal of adult education programme of 'Pragati Centre' of the Department of Home Science Extension and Communication, Faculty of Home Science, The M.S. University Baroda in the year 2003-2004.

Background Information of the Respondents

Table 6: Percentage Distribution According to the Background Information of the Respondents

N=125

Sr. No.	*Variables*	*Percentage (%)*
1.	Age	
	i) Young	64.0
	ii) Old	36.0
2.	Educational level	
	i) Low	74.4
	ii) Medium	12.0
	iii) High	13.6
3.	Regularity in attendance	
	i) Regular	62.4
	ii) Irregular	37.6
4.	Personality dimension	
	i) Introvert	39.2
	ii) Extrovert	60.8
5.	Motivation to learn	
	i) High motivation	14.4
	ii) Low motivation	85.6

Table 6 shows that 64 per cent of the respondents were young and 36 per cent of the respondents were old. It is also seen that more than 70 per cent of the respondents were having low level of education, whereas, nearly 14 per cent of the respondents were highly educated. Nearly 40 per cent of the respondents were introverts whereas 60 per cent of the respondents were extroverts. A majority of the respondents were regular in attending the adult education programme. However about 85 per cent of the respondents were having low motivation. Further, nearly 15 per cent of the respondents were found to be highly motivated.

Table 7: Percentage Distribution Showing Other Characteristics Related to Background Information of the Respondents

N=125

Sr. No.	*Other Characteristics*	*Percentage (%)*
1.	Caste	
	i) General	44.0
	ii) Schedule caste	41.6
	iii) Schedule trible	14.4
2.	Religion	
	i) Hindu	77.6
	ii) Muslim	16.0
	iii) Christian	4.8
	iv) Any other	1.6
3.	Type of house	64.8
	i) Puckka house	32.0
	ii) Kaccha house	3.2
	iii) Other	
4.	Type of the family	
	i) Joint family	71.2
	ii) Nuclear family	28.8

Table 7 reveals that an almost equal percentage of the respondents were from the general caste and schedule caste, whereas, 14 per cent of the respondents were from scheduled tribes. A high majority, i.e., nearly 70 per cent of the respondents were Hindus, whereas, 16 per cent of the respondents were Muslims, nearly 5 per cent of them were Christians whereas only 2 per cent of the respondents tell in the other category, like Parsi or Sikh. Nearly 65 per cent of the respondents lived in puckka houses, 32 per cent of them were living in kaccha houses and only 3 per cent of the respondents fell in other category, like living in huts. A majority, i.e., 71 per cent of the respondents were having joint families whereas nearly 30 per cent of the respondents were living in nuclear families.

Table 8: Percentage Distribution of the Respondents Showing the Number of Family Members

N=125

Sr. No.	*Other Characteristics*	*Percentage (%)*
1.	Total number of family members	
	i) 1-3 members	10.4
	ii) 4-6 members	67.2
	iii) 7-9 members	17.6
	iv) 10-12 members	4.8
2.	i) Number of male members in the family	
	a) 1-2 members	48.0
	b) 3-4 members	41.6
	c) 5 and more	10.4
	ii) Number of female members in the family	
	a) 1-2 members	40.0
	b) 3-4 members	50.4
	c) 5 and more	9.6

It is seen from Table 8 that a majority, i.e., 67 per cent of the respondents had four to six family members, whereas, nearly 20 per cent of the respondents had seven to 9 family members, ten per cent of the respondents had one to three family members and only five per cent of the respondents had ten to twelve family members. Table 8 also shows that an almost equal percentage of the respondents had three to four male members and one to two female members in their family, whereas, 48 per cent of the respondents had one to two male members and an almost equal percentage of the respondents had five and more male and female members in their family; the remaining 50 per cent of the respondents had three to four female family members.

Table 9: Percentage Distribution of the Respondents Showing the Occupation Related Information

N=125

Sr. No.	*Other Characteristics*	*Percentage (%)*
1.	Occupation of the head of the family	
	i) Service	43.2
	ii) Labour	38.4
	iii) Business	11.2
	iv) Any other	7.2
2.	Number of earning family members	
	i) 1 member	60.0
	ii) 2 members	28.0
	iii) 3 members	10.4
	iv) 4 members	1.6
3.	Total income of the family	
	i) Low income group	50.0
	ii) Middle income group	30.4
	iii) High income group	19.2

It is seen from Table 9 that 43 per cent of the respondents had service, 38 per cent labour and 11 per cent of the respondent's head of the family had business as the main occupation. It is also evident from Table 9 that majority of the families had only one earning member in the family, 28 per cent of the respondents had two earning members, whereas, 10 per cent of the respondents had three earning members and nearly 20 per cent of the respondents had four earning members in the family.

Table 10 reveals that a majority, i.e., nearly 85 per cent of the respondents had Gujarati medium, nearly 9 per cent of the respondents had Hindi medium, nearly 6 per cent of the respondents had English medium in schools/colleges. However, 0.08 per cent of the respondents had other medium like Marathi, Urdu, etc., in schools/colleges.

Table 10 : Percentage Distribution of the Respondents Showing the Education Related Information

N=125

Sr. No.	*Medium of Instruction in Schools / Colleges*	*Percentage*
1.	Gujarati	84.8
2.	Hindi	8.8
3.	English	5.6
4.	Any other	0.8

Table 11 : Percentage Distribution of the Respondents According to the Marital Status

N=125

Sr. No.	*Marital Status*	*Percentage*
1.	Unmarried	60.8
2.	Married	37.6
3.	Separated	1.6
4.	Widowed	—

Table 11 shows that a majority, i.e., nearly 61 per cent of the respondents were unmarried, whereas, nearly 38 per cent of the respondents were married and nearly 2 per cent of the respondents were separated.

Table 12 shows that a majority, i.e., nearly 82 per cent of the respondents were not employed whereas, 18 per cent of the respondents were employed.

Table 12: Percentage Distribution of the Respondents Showing the Employment Status of the Respondents

N=125

Sr. No.	*Other Characteristics*	*Percentage*
1.	Not employed	81.6
2.	Employed	18.4

Table 13 shows that a high majority, i.e., nearly 80 per cent of the respondents were self-motivated to be employed, whereas, 15 per cent of the respondents were encouraged by their friends and remaining equal per centage of the respondents were encouraged to be employed by their husband and parents. It is also evident from Table 13 that almost 74 per cent of the respondents had a low salary, whereas, 26 per cent of the respondents had high salary.

Table 13: Percentage Distribution of the Respondents Showing the Employment-related Information

N=23

Sr. No.	*Other Characteristics*	*Percentage*
1.	Adult learners were encouraged to be employed by:	
	i) On their own	78.3
	ii) Friends	13.0
	iii) Husband	4.3
	iv) Parents	4.3
	v) In-laws	—
2.	Salary	
	i) Low salary	73.9
	ii) High salary	26.0
3.	Work experience	
	i) More experience	52.1
	ii) Less experience	47.8
4.	Working hours	
	i) Less hours	56.5
	ii) More hours	43.5

Table 14: Percentage Distribution of the Respondents Showing the Number of Years of Attending the Adult Education Programme at 'Pragati Centre'

N=125

Sr. No.	*Number of Years of Attending the Adult Education Programme*	*Percentage*
1.	One year	82.4
2.	Two years	11.2
3.	Three years	0.8
4.	Four years	4.8
5.	More than four years	0.8

It can be further seen from Table 13 that an almost equal percentage of the respondents had more or less working experience, whereas, 56 per cent of the respondents work for less hours and 43 per cent of the respondents work for more hours.

Table 15: Percentage Distribution of the Respondents Showing the Distance from Home to 'Pragati Centre' and Mode of Transportation

N=125

Sr. No.	*Other Characteristics*	*Percentage*
1.	Distance from home to 'Pragati Centre'	
	i) Less than 1 km	30.4
	ii) 1-2 kms	26.4
	iii) 3-4 kms	6.4
	iv) 5-6 kms	20.0
	v) More than 6 kms	16.8
2.	Mode of transportation	
	i) On foot	51.2
	ii) By autorickshaw	36.0
	iii) By bus	9.6
	iv) By cycle	1.6
	v) By own vehicle	1.6

Table 15 reveals that 30 per cent of the respondents had less than one kilometre distance from home to 'Pragati Centre', 26 per cent of the respondents had one to 2 kilometres distance, six per cent of the respondents had three to four kilometers distance whereas, 20 per cent of the respondents had five to six kilometers and nearly 17 per cent of the respondents had more than six kilometres distance from home to 'Pragati Centre'.

Table 14 reveals that 82 per cent of the respondents had attended the Adult Education Programme for 1 year, 11 per cent of the respondents had attended for 2 years, nearly one per cent of the respondents had attended for 3 years, nearly 5 per cent of the respondents had attended for 4 years and again nearly one per cent of the respondents had attended the adult education programme for more than four years.

Little more than 50 per cent of the respondents came on foot to 'Pragati Centre', 36 per cent of the respondents came by autorickshaw, whereas, nearly 10 per cent of the respondents came by bus, nearly 2 per cent of the respondents came by cycle and by their own vehicle to 'Pragati Centre'.

Table 16 reveals that 35 per cent of the respondents were encouraged by their friends, 27 per cent of the respondents were encouraged on their own, 24 per cent of them were encouraged by their family members, whereas, nearly 10 per cent of the respondents were encouraged by local leader and 4 per cent of the respondents were encouraged by their relatives to join the adult education classes.

Table 16: Percentage Distribution of the Respondents Showing the Persons who Encouraged in Joining the Adult Education Classes

N=125

Sr. No.	*Persons who Encouraged in Joining the Adult Education Classes*	*Percentage*
1.	Friends	35.2
2.	Your own wish	27.2
3.	Family members	24.0
4.	Local leaders	9.6
5.	Relatives	4.0

Table 17 shows that only 8 per cent of the respondents had faced opposition in the family to join the adult education classes.

Table 17: Percentage Distribution of the Respondents Showing the Persons who Opposed the Participation in the Adult Education Programme

N=125

Sr. No.		*Other Characteristics*	*Percentage*
1.	i)	Not faced opposition	92.0
	ii)	Faced opposition	8.0
2.		Person who opposed (N=10)	
	i)	Family members	50.0
	ii)	Husband	30.0
	iii)	Relatives	10.0
	iii)	Others	10.0

Fifty per cent of the respondents faced opposition by their family members, 30 per cent of the respondents faced opposition by their husband, whereas, 10 per cent of the respondents faced opposition by their relatives and others, like local leaders or friends.

Overall Opinions Reported by Adult Learners

Table 18: Overall Opinions of the Respondents Regarding the 'Adult Education Programme'

N=125

Sr. No.	*Extent of Opinions*	*Percentage*
1.	High	77.6
2.	Moderate	22.4
3.	Low	—

Table 18 shows that nearly 78 per cent of the respondents had overall high opinion regarding the Adult Education Programme, whereas, 22 per cent of the respondents had moderate opinion regarding the Adult Education Programme, and it is interesting to find that nobody had a low opinion regarding the Adult Education Programme.

This implies that the Adult Education Programme was well planned and executed by the instructors and teacher supervisors, which resulted in an effective adult education programme. It also reflects the favourable attitude of the adult learners towards the Adult Education Programme.

Overall Opinions Reported by Adult Learners According to the Variables

Table 19 reveals that an almost equal percentage of the respondents had high and moderate opinion regarding the Adult Education Programme with respect to the age, educational level, personality dimension and motivation to learn, whereas, those who were regular had a high opinion in comparison to those who were irregular in attending the adult education classes.

Table 19: Overall Opinion of the Respondents About 'Adult Education Programme' According to the Variables

N=125

Sr. No.	*Variables*	*High (%)*	*Moderate (%)*	*Low (%)*
1.	Age			
	– Young (N=80)	80.0	20.0	–
	– Old (N=45)	73.3	26.7	–
2.	Educational level			
	– Low (N=93)	78.5	21.5	–
	– Medium (N=15)	73.3	26.7	–
	– High (N=17)	76.5	23.5	–
3.	Regularity in attendance			
	– Regular (N=78)	83.3	16.7	–
	– Irregular (N=47)	68.1	31.9	–
4.	Personality Dimension			
	– Introvert (N=49)	73.5	26.5	–
	– Extrovert (N=76)	80.3	19.7	–
5.	Motivation to learn			
	– High motivation (N=18)	72.2	27.8	–
	– Low motivation (N=107)	78.5	21.5	–

Item-wise Opinion Reported by Adult Learners

Opinion About 'Education 'Aspect of the Programme

Table 20: Item-wise Intensity Indices Showing the Opinion of the Respondent about 'Education' Aspect of the Programme.

N=125

Sr.No	*Items*	*I.I*
1.	Adult Education Programme provides the knowledge, which is useful in day-to-day life.	2.66
2.	Adult Education Programme helps in increasing the literacy level of the learners.	2.66
3.	Adult Education Programme taught many things besides the content, eg. Discipline, handling different situations etc.	2.55

4.	Adult Education Programme fulfilled the purpose for which the programme was joined.	2.55
5.	The content taught is remembered even after the completion of the class.	2.50
6.	Adult Education Programme gives different ideas of self-employment.	2.44
7.	The content taught in the class is of no use as no further guidance is given to what should be done afterwards.	2.40
8.	Curriculum of the Adult Education Programme is not worth because women indulge only in gossiping.	2.29
9.	The content taught in the Adult Education Programme was difficult to understand.	2.24
10	The content taught in the Adult Education Programme had too many ideas, which was confusing.	1.46

It is seen from Table 20 that respondents had opined to a great extent that adult education programme provided the knowledge, which is useful in day-to-day life, and it also increased their literacy level, whereas, the respondents had a moderate opinion regarding the adult education content as many things were taught besides the content. The content taught was remembered even after the completion of the class. Adult Education Programme gave different ideas of self-employment,; there was no use of content as no further guidance was given; curriculum was not worth attending as women only indulged in gossiping, and the content was difficult to understand. This implies that the adult learners were concerned for their self-development to a moderate level.

Opinion about Self-development Aspect of the Programme

Table 21 reveals that all the respondents had opined to a moderate level, that after attending the adult education programme they had developed a feeling of having an ambition in life; they started taking decisions in the family matters; they developed the feeling of independence; they became open in sharing ideas with others; they became confident in interacting with others; they developed the ability of communicating with different people; they started putting; they decisions into action; they became open in sharing ideas with others, became strong to oppose the injustice and they started discussing and solving the problems of community.

Table 21: Item-wise Intensity Indices Showing the Opinion of the Respondent about Self-development Aspect of the Programme

N=125

Sr.No	*Items*	*I.I*
	The Adult Education Programme:	2.66
1	Developed a feeling of having an ambition in life.	2.52
2.	Started taking decisions in the family matters.	2.50
3.	Developed the feeling of independence.	2.49
4.	Became open in sharing ideas with others.	2.49
5.	Became confident in interacting with others.	2.48
6.	Developed the ability of communicating with different people.	2.45
7.	Started putting decisions into action.	2.43
8.	Became open in sharing ideas with others.	2.39
9.	Became strong to oppose the injustice.	2.30
10	Started discussing and solving the problems of community.	2.06

Opinion about *Health* Aspect of the Programme

Table 22: Item-wise Intensity Indices Showing the Opinion of the Respondent about 'Health' Aspect of the Programme

N=125

Sr.No	*Items*	*I.I*
1.	Became curious to find new recipes.	2.7U
2.	Started cooking new recipes keeping in mind its nutritive value.	2.65
3.	Became concerned about the nutritious diet of family members.	2.6?
4.	Became concerned about health of family members.	2.55
5.	Became concerned about diet.	2.55

It can be seen from Table 22 that respondents were very much concerned to find out about new recipes, trying out new recipes and also keeping a check on its nutritive value and diet of their family members, whereas, the respondents were concerned to some extent only about their own diet and health.

Opinion about *Creativity* Aspect of the Programme

It can be seen from the Table 23 that the respondents had started collecting innovative ideas for making creative articles, created beautiful articles out of waste materials, started thinking that income can be generated by making creative articles, decorated home with different creative articles or showpieces and started making creative articles such as lampshade, artificial flowers etc to some extent.

Table 23: Item-wise Intensity Indices Showing the Opinion of the Respondent about Creativity Aspect of the Programme.

N=125

Sr.No	*Items*	*I.I*
1.	Started collecting innovative ideas for making creative articles.	2.41
2.	Created beautiful articles out of waste materials.	2.40
3.	Started thinking that income can be generated by making creative articles.	2.14
4.	Decorated home with different creative articles or showpieces.	2.04
5.	Started making creative articles such as lampshade, artificial flowers etc.	1.90

Opinions about *Instructors* of the Programme

It can be seen from Table 24 that the respondents had very high opinion regarding the instructors who taught them in the Adult Education Programme. They reported that the instructors were punctual in the adult education classes; they were helping and caring, their language was clearly understood; they were confident while conducting the classes; they gave solutions to queries; their voice was clear and loud; they taught according to the pace of learning; they had enthusiastically discussed their ideas and experiences regarding AIDS, reproductive system, etc., they were friendly in nature; they gave equal opportunities to all to participate in the adult education programme; they they had taught in an interesting manner; they were able to maintain the discipline in the adult education classes; they were sympathetic; they described the same thing in different ways to develop a clear understanding and were impartial with the learners.

Opinions about *Physical* Aspect of the Programme

It can be seen from Table 25 that respondents had high opinion regarding the physical aspect of the Adult Education Programme. They reported that seating arrangement was comfortable for them; there was no suffocation as proper ventilation was there; there was adequate light to see properly; they could conveniently view the demonstrations conducted in the Adult Education Programme and timings of the classes were also convenient for them.

Table 24: Item-wise Intensity Indices Showing the Opinion of the Respondent about *Instructors* of the Adult Education Programme of 'Pragati Centre'

N=125

Sr.No	*Items*	*I.I*
1.	Were punctual in the adult education classes.	2.87
2.	Were helping and caring.	2.84
3.	Language was clearly understood.	2.78
4.	Were confident while conducting the Adult Education Programme.	2.76
5.	Gave solutions to queries.	2.75
6.	Voice was clear and loud.	2.74
7.	Taught according to the pace of learning.	2.74
8.	Enthusiastically discussed their ideas and experiences, e.g., regarding AIDS, reproductive system, etc.	2.74
9.	Were friendly.	2.73

10.	Gave equal opportunities to all to participate in the Adult Education Programme.	2.72
11.	Taught in an interesting manner.	2.70
12.	Were able to maintain the discipline in the adult education classes.	2.68
13.	Were sympathetic.	2.66
14.	Described the same thing in different ways to develop a clear understanding.	2.64
15.	Were impartial with the learners.	2.24

It can be seen from Table 26 that respondents had a very high opinion regarding teaching aids, which were used by the instructors, and according to their opinion teaching aids were well prepared.

Table 27 shows that specimens, posters, photograph were found to be the most effective teaching aids, whereas, the respondents had a moderate opinion regarding flashcards, models and flipcharts.

Table 25: Item-wise Intensity Indices Showing the Opinions of the Respondents about *Physical* Aspect of 'Pragati Centre'

N=125

Sr.No	*Items*	*I.I*
1.	Comfortable sitting arrangement.	2.84
2.	Proper ventilation.	2.83
3.	Adequate light to see clearly.	2.83
4.	Convenient to have a full view of demonstration.	2.76
5.	Timings of the classes were convenient.	2.69

Opinion about *Methods and Materials*

Table 26: Item-wise Intensity Indices Showing the Opinion of the Respondents about *Methods and Materials*

N=125

Sr.No	*Items*	*I.I*
1.	Several teaching aids were used by the instructors.	2.97
2.	Teaching aids were well prepared.	2.97

Tabie 27: Item-wise Intensity Indices Showing the Opinions of the Respondents about the Effectiveness of *Teaching Aids*

N=125

Sr.No	*Teaching Aids*	*I.I*
1.	Specimens	2.78
2.	Posters	2.78
3.	Photographs	2.72
4.	Flashcards	2.50
5.	Models	2.48
6.	Flipcharts	2.34

Table 28 shows that the respondents had, high opinion regarding discussion, demonstration and drama, whereas, the respondents had a moderate opinion regarding educational talk and workshop method.

After having learnt it through demonstrations and workshops the respondents had made the following recipes and articles at home.

Table 28: Item-wise Intensity Indices Showing the Opinions of the Respondents about the Effectiveness of Teaching Methods

N=125

Sr.No	*Teaching Methods*	*I.I*
1.	Discussion	2.66
2.	Demonstration	2.65
3.	Drama	2.62
4.	Educational talk	2.51
5.	Workshop	2.38

Recipes made by the respondents were gold coin, papad ka samosa, veg., pizza, bread idli, cake, American roll, khajoor ki puran puri, Chinese roll, bread macroni, rasraj, anarsa, malbari kari, veg. roll, veg. lollipop, veg. strip, paneertikka masala, kheer, mung ki patis, sandwich, veg. pav, apple jam, vegetable candy, khajoor ki cholocolate, kaju vada, punjabi korma, and aaloo vada.

Articles made by the respondents were wax basket, pot decoration, flowerpot, painting, toran, wall piece, bandhini, tablelamp, ceramic articles and decorative candles.

Overall Differences in the Opinions of the Adult Learner According to the Variables

It can be seen from Table 29 that regularity in attendance was found to be significant at 5 per cent level of significance. So, the null hypotheses that there is no significant difference in the opinion and regularity in attendance was not accepted.

Age, educational level, personality dimension and motivation to learn were not found to be significant at 5 per cent level of significance. So, the null hypotheses that there will be no significant difference in the opinion with respect to the age, educational level, and personality dimension and motivation to learn is accepted. This implies that adult learners of different age group, different educational level, different personality and motivation had similar opinion regarding the adult education programme, whereas, regular and irregular adult learners were differed in their opinions.

Table 29 : Overall Differences in the Opinions of the Respondents Regarding the Adult Education Programme with Respect to the Selected Variables

N=125

Sr.No.	*Variables*	*Chi-square Value*	*df*	*Significant at 5% Level of Significance*
1.	Age	.73638	1	.39082 (NS)
2.	Educational level	.21239	2	.89925 (NS)
3.	Regularity in attendance	3.92294	1	.04763 (S*)
4.	Personality dimension	.79106	1	.37378 (NS)
5.	Motivation to learn	.34986	1	.55419 (NS)

NS = Not significant, S* = Significant at 0.05 level

Reasons for Not Attending the Adult Education Classes

It can be seen from Table 30 that very small percentage of the respondents had reasons for not attending the adult education classes, whereas, at the same time it is also evident from the table

30 that the place was unknown where the classes were conducted, and it was expensive to come to 'Pragati Centre'. These were found to be the major reasons for not attending the adult education classes. Other reported reasons for not attending the classes were that they had to go for part-time/full time job at the same time of the adult education classes; they had to look after one of the family member who was sick at home; the activities of the adult education classes were not informed to them; they had to look after a young child in the family; the exact time of the class was unknown to them; they thought that others have much more creativity then they have; they were tired because of household work; the timings of the adult education classes were not convenient; they had to go for other classes at the same time, like beauty parlour, stitching classes, etc., they thought that it was not worth attending the classes, as no job opportunity was there even after attending the adult education classes; they were sick when adult education classes were going on; it was the time when their children returned home from school and when their husbands came home from the office these were reported by a small percentage of the respondents.

Table 30 : Item-wise Percentage Distribution of the Respondents According to the Reasons for Not Attending the Adult Education Classes.

N = *125*

Sr. No.	*Items*	*Yes (%)*	*No (%)*
1.	The place where the classes are conducted was unknown.	54.4	45.6
2.	It was expensive to come to 'Pragati Centre' because of long distance from home to 'Pragati Centre'.	44.8	55.2
3.	Had to go for part-time/full time job at the same time of the adult education classes.	40.0	60.0
4.	Had to look after one of the family members who was sick at home.	39.2	60.8
5.	The activities of the adult education classes were not informed in advance.	38.4	61.6

6.	Had to look after a young child in the family.	37.6	62.4
7.	The exact time of the class was unknown	36.0	64.0
8.	It was thought that others have much creativity.	36.0	64.0
9.	Tiredness because of household work.	33.6	66.4
10.	Timings of the adult education classes were not convenient.	32.0	68.0
11.	Had to go for other classes at the same time like beauty parlour, stitching classes, etc.	27.2	72.8
12.	It is not worth to attend the classes, as no job opportunity is there after attending the adult education classes.	24.8	75.2
13.	Had sickness when adult education classes were going on.	19.2	80.8
14.	It was the time of children to return home from the school.	17.6	82.4
15.	It was the time of husband to come home from the office.	13.6	86.4

SUGGESTIONS OBTAINED FROM ADULT LEARNERS, UBS/UCD COMMUNITY VOLUNTEERS, TEACHER SUPERVISORS

Table 31 reveals that majority of the respondents agreed to a great extent that computer education should be provided. This tables also shows that more opportunities for self-expression, library facility and further guidance should be provided were suggested by the majority of the respondents. It is also evident from this table that 70 per cent of the respondents were suggested that a children centre facility should be provided and exhibition should be put up for the products made in the adult education classes. Nearly 65 per cent of the respondent suggested that adequate transport arrangement should be made and 60 per cent of the respondent suggested that awareness regarding marketing strategies should be provided.

Table 32 reveals that thoughtful attention to the needs of the learners, openness which eases the expression of views and professional guidance should be provided were suggested by the majority of the Urban Basic Services and Urban Community

Development Project's Community Volunteers. Nearly 65 per cent of them suggested that adequate transport arrangement should be made and a childcare center facility should be provided so that women can attend the adult education programme free from the worry of their children. Further, 50 per cent of the Urban Basic Services and Urban Community Development Project's Community volunteers suggested that awareness regarding marketing strategies, computer education and library facility should be provided.

Table 31 : Percentage Distribution Showing the Suggestions of the Adult Learners Regarding the Adult Education Programme

N=125

Sr.No	*Items*	*Great Extent (%)*	*Some Extent (%)*	*Less Extent (%)*
1.	Computer education should be provided.	82.4	16.0	1.6
2.	More opportunities should be provided for self-expression.	75.2	19.2	5.6
3.	A library facility should be provided which would develop reading habits and increase knowledge.	74.4	21.6	4.0
4.	Further guidance to what should be done afterwards can make the programme more meaningful.	73.6	24.0	2.4
5.	A childcare centre facility should be provided so that women can attend the adult education programme free from the worry of their children.	70.0	24.8	4.8
6.	Exhibition can be put up for the products made in the adult education classes.	68.8	24.8	6.4
7.	Adequate transport arrangement should be made	64.8	28.0	7.2

(Contd...)

(Contd...)

8. Awareness regarding marketing strategies should be provided to sell the products.60.0	35.2	4.8	
9. Aspect of the programme you think needs renewal.			
a) Management of the programme	44.0	36.8	28.8
b) Instructors training	28.8	27.2	34.4

Awareness regarding marketing strategies should be provided to sell the products was suggested by all the teacher supervisors of the Adult Education Programme. A majority, i.e., 75 per cent of the teacher supervisors suggested that thoughtful attention should be given to the needs of the learners; there should be an openness which eases the expression of views on the part of the adult learners; a library facility should be provided which would develop reading habits and increase knowledge; a childcare centre facility should be provided so that women can attend the adult education programme free from the worry of their children, and professional guidance should be given to the adult learners.

Table 32: Percentage Distribution Showing the Suggestions of the UBS/UCD Community Volunteers and Teacher Supervisors Regarding the Adult Education Programme.

		UBS/UCD N=6			*Supervisors N=4*		
Sr. No.	*Items*	*GE*	*SE*	*LE*	*GE*	*SE*	*LE*
1.	Thoughtful attention should be given to the needs of the learners.	100	–	–	75.0	25.0	–
2.	There should be an openness, which eases the expression of views on the part of the adult learners.	83.3	16.6	–	75.0	25.0	–
3.	Awareness regarding marketing strategies						

(Contd...)

(Contd...)

should be provided to sell the products.	50.0	16.6	33.3	100	–	–
4. Computer education should be provided.	50.0	16.6	33.3	50.0	50.0	–
5. Adequate transport arrangement should be made.	66.6	33.3	–	50.0	50.0	–
6. A library facility should be provided which would develop reading habits and increase knowledge.	50.0	33.3	16.6	75.0	–	25.0
7. A childcare centre facility should be provided so that women can attend the adult education programme free from the worry of their children.	66.6	16.6	16.6	75.0	~	25.0
8. Professional guidance should be given to the adult learners.	83.3	16.6	–	75.0	25.0	~
9. Aspects of the programme you think need renewal						
a) Management of the programme	16.6	33.3	50.0	–	–	100
b) Instructors training	50.0	50.0	–	–	25.0	75.0

5

Significance of Adult Education

This chapter presents the discussion of the major findings of the study of an appraisal of adult education programme of 'Pragati Centre' of the Department of Home Science Extension and Communication, Faculty of Home Science, The M.S. University, Baroda in the year 2003-2004.

Background Information

It was found that a majority of the adult learners had a low educational level. The reason may be that adult learners had many responsibilities at home like taking care of siblings, cooking food, etc., or may be their parents feared sending their daughters for further education in a school/college as the atmosphere is such where parents feel insecure about their girls. Parents might have also felt that if their daughters were to be highly educated it would be difficult for them to find a suitable match.

Attendance was not compulsory yet a majority of the adult learners regularly attended the adult education classes. This shows that the adult learners are very keen to learn. They may have wanted to study further and increase their knowledge, as the content of the programme might be of interest to them, encouraging them to attend the classes regularly. The other reason may be that they had a good company of friends with whom they enjoyed and regularly attended the classes. A majority of the adult learners were found to be extroverts. The reason might be that they were very enthusiastic, active and expressive which promoted active participation in the Adult Education Programme. Similar findings had been reported by Reddy (1986) who asserted that the success of any adult education programme largely depends on the target group's participation in it. Their participation in turn is determined by their personality characteristics. The personality characteristics which were found to promote active participation in the programme are cheerfulness, talkativeness, impulsiveness, practical and realistic outlook, adaptable nature, concern for others, ability to work in a team, confidence in self, capacity to deal with things, accompanied by coolness, desire for social approval and extroversion. It was found that the majority of the adult learners had low motivation to learn. They probably had not got the opportunity to express their views in front of others. An opportunity for self-expression encourages and motivates a person and generates confidence when the person's views are appreciated by others. Hence, it might be possible that the adult learners got a chance but they were not appreciated by others. Their past experiences may have been such that they were demotivated to learn further.

Another reason could be that as it is a male-dominated society adult learners might have feared that their freedom would be restricted if they showed their motivation and desire to learn. Hence, it was better that they had no motivation to learn. Another reason could be that continuous learning builds motivation to learn, but these adults were unable to continue their education. Hence, their motivation suffered because of a long break in education. It was found that the majority of the adult learners were Hindus. The reason may be that the target had come in groups for the Adult Education Programme and a possibility that many groups were exclusively Hindu girls. However, 16 per cent of the adult learners were Muslims. The reason may be that as Muslims follow the purdah system, parents might have felt secure in sending their daughters to the Home Science Faculty because it is a girls, college. Secondly, the Faculty of Home Science is close to many Muslims communities, like Nizampura, Fatehgunj, Kamatipura from where around 16 per cent of Muslim girls might have come. It was found that the majority of the respondents belonged to the joint family. The reason may be, as they were poor and living in the urban slum area, it was difficult to own a house which was very expensive to buy and everybody could not afford an independent house. So, it might be possible that they lived under one umbrella only. Another reason could be that people get married at an early age, which increases the number of family members in each household. It was found that the majority of the respondents' heads of the family were either in service or in labour force. The reason may be that as they were poor, living in the urban area, it was expensive and difficult, to get a place for establishing one's own business, as it require a lot of investment. There are many ups and downs a person has to face in business, as it is very risky, so it might be possible that they could not afford to take risk in business and felt secure in taking up a job or earning as daily wage labourers.

The majority of the adult learners had only one family member who was earning, probably because other male members were either too young and thus studying in a school/college or they were too old to go out to work. It might also be possible that female members were not allowed to go out to take up jobs. However, a few women were found to be earning. The reason may be that they had no male members in the family or the male members were unable to get employment. It might be possible that women were forced to earn or may be they wanted to be independent and have their own identity.

It was found that 50 per cent of the adult learners belonged to the low-income group. This could be attributed to the adult learners belonging to the joint family where only one family member was earning. It might also be possible that those who were earning were not much educated. Hence, they were getting low wages, as there is a lot of competition in the job market in today's world. Even the educated don't get employment, and it is very difficult to survive in this competitive world. Hence, it might be possible that even if they are educated, there is a little value tothat education in the job market and therefore they end up getting low salaries or low wages.

Further, it was found that the majority of the adult learners had Gujarati medium of instruction in their schools/colleges. It may be because that people living in Baroda slums were more comfortable in sending their children to municipal schools where the medium of instruction is Gujarati. Children are much influenced by their parents and the home environment, and they learn what their parents teach them. Hence, it might be possible that the parents of adult learners had low education with a Gujarati background, so this could be other reason that adult learners had Gujarati medium in their schools/colleges. It might also be possible that as they were poor, belonging to the low income group, their parents could not afford to send them to English medium schools where they had to pay high fees for education, buy expensive books, pay high tuition fees. Hence, it might be possible that they were sending their daughters to the government schools/colleges, which had Gujarati as a medium of instruction.

It was also found that the majority of the adult learners were not employed as they were young and also had a low level of education, which is not enough to get an employment. It might also be possible that they were capable of getting an employment but as it is a male-dominated society, the family members may not have allowed them to get employment. Moreover, the adult learners had a low level of education, so it might be possible that they were getting employment, which had a low status in society. Hence, they might not have liked to be employed. It was found that only 18 per cent of the adult learners were employed and a majority of them had employment because of their own motivation. The reason may be that they wanted to be a helping hand to their parents by adding some extra income, as they were very concerned about the income status of the family. Another reason could be that the adult learners did not like to be dependent on others, as they wanted to be independent and to have their own income and identity.

A majority of the adult learners were getting low salaries as they had a low level of education. It was found that a majority of the adult learners were working for a very few hours. The reason could be that they had to reach home early and take care of the home-related responsibilities, which they could not afford to neglect. The demand of the job itself may not require long hours of work like the job of a helper. It was found that majority of the adult learners had been attending the Adult Education Programme at 'Pragati Centre' for one year. The reason may be that every year UBS/UCD Community volunteers approach different slum communities so that maximum slums could be covered and maximum people could get the benefit of the Adult Education Programme which is conducted every year in the Department of Home Science Extension and Communication, Faculty of Home Science.

However, a few of the adult learners were attending the Adult Education Programme at 'Pragati Centre' for more than one year probably because they were more confident in attending the adult education classes as they were able to manage the time without neglecting household responsibilities. It might also be possible that they enjoyed attending the adult education classes as they had made friends while attending the programme and got used to coming to 'Pragati Centre'. It was also found that a little more then 50 per cent of the adult learners came 'on foot' to the 'Pragati Centre' to attend the programme. They might have wished to save money. Secondly, 50 per cent of the adult learners lived within one to two kilometre distances from 'Pragati Centre'.

However, some of the adult learners came by autorickshaw. It might be possible that they came half way on foot and covered the other half way by a shared autorickshaw, which was not very expensive for them. Another reason for coming by an autorickshaw may be that there was no bus stop near the area where they were living or maybe the adult learners found that a lot of time was being wasted while waiting for bus on the bus stop. A little more than one-third of the adult learners were encouraged to join the adult education classes by their friends, which may be because they wanted the company of their friends or may be their parents were not allowing them to go out alone. Another reason can be that a person enjoys more in a friendly atmosphere; they feel free and comfortable. Hence the company of a friend was stressed by them.

However, a few adult learners were encouraged by their own to join the adult education classes, probably because they wanted to increase their knowledge. Or maybe they thought that it was a good opportunity to go to college to attend the classes which otherwise was not possible for them. It was interesting to find that a high majority of the adult learners had not faced any opposition in the family to join the adult education classes, which may be because their family members knew that the classes are conducted in the Faculty of Home Science where there are only females which made them feel secure in sending their daughters. In spite of the fact that a majority of the adult learners belonged to low income group, they were not restricted or discouraged from going ahead to attend the classes as there were no fee or expenses to join the classes.

Aspect-wise Opinion Regarding the Adult Education Programme

The findings of the study revealed that the overall majority of the adult learner had a high opinion of the Adult Education Programme may be because the programme was so well planned and executed by the instructors and teacher supervisors which resulted in an effective Adult Education Programme. Another reason could be that attitude towards a particular thing affects the response towards it. Acceptance of anything to a great extent depends upon the attitude of people towards it. Hence, it might be possible that the adult learners had a positive attitude towards the Adult Education Programme, which might be a major factor in generating a high opinion of the Adult Education Programme.

Patel (1981) had also reported similar findings in her study that a majority of the women from the weaker section of Baroda had a favourable attitude towards the non-formal education programme. The other findings of the education aspect of the programme revealed that the adult learners knowledge as a high priority, which was useful in day-to-day life. Further the Adult Education Programme helped in increasing the literacy level of the learners. This finding shows that the adult learners benefited from the Adult Education Programme in terms of increase in knowledge. The reason may be that the contents of the programme were of their interest. So, it can be said that the success of the programme is largely dependent upon the content, which is selected by the teacher supervisors and instructors. Hence the needs and interests of the adult learners should be kept in mind while selecting the content for the Adult Education Programme. Further, it was also found that the adult learners had moderate opinion about many other things being taught besides the content, like discipline, handlings different situations and so on. It might be because they learnt it through second-hand experience. As researches have proved, a person learns more through first-hand experiences. So, the instructors should give more opportunities to adult learners to handle different situations. However, they also had moderate opinions about the effect of the content taught after the completion of the classes. One of the reasons could be that the women were so much occupied with their household work that indirect benefit in the long run may not have interested them much. Or may be they were not in touch with the education, so they could not recall or remember the contents much after the class.

The findings of the "self-development aspect" of the programme revealed that the adult learners had moderate opinion about it. That means the adult learners were concerned about their self-development to a moderate level which is a very positive sign of development, in spite of having low education, low income and coming from poor families, they showed the willingness to strive for their own self-development. It was an inbuilt wish in the adult learners. The reason could be many, maybe they understood that this is a rapidly changing world towards new developments. To survive in this world a person has to accept and adopt change. Hence, they wanted to be in the line of fulfilling the demand. So there is a change in their attitudes, actions and beliefs so as to be good citizens of a nation and contribute to the family indirectly by developing themselves in spite of having low educational status.

Another reason could be that the adult learners had interacted with those who were concerned for their development and who had high ambition in their life or could take correct decision in life. The adult learners might have been influenced by those people and may have wanted to be like them. As the adult learners were concerned for their self-development to a moderate level, it can be said that the instructors still have a scope to encourage them further by improving in delivery of instructions, actions, ideas, thoughts and experiences. The instructors should make the adult learners realise that a person should be capable of facing the problem and handling different situations of life and that can be done by realising the need and concern for their "Self-development".

Further, the findings of the "health aspect" of the programme revealed that the adult learners were concerned to a great extent to know about new recipes, try out new recipes and also keep a check on nutritive value of the diet of their family members. The probable reason may be that they were very much concerned about their health as everybody wants to look good and healthy. As the people of slum areas are generally malnourished and often fall sick, maybe they wanted to take precautions by giving nutritious diets to their family members. Another reason could be that they liked to serve new recipes to their family members to break the monotony of daily routine diet. This finding of the study implies that the adult learners like to learn new recipes. Hence, the instructors, while selecting the items for food demonstration for the adult education programme, should keep in mind that it should be new and attractive, it should be of low cost and should have a good amount of nutritive value.

The findings of the "creativity aspect" of the programme revealed that the adult learners had moderate opinion regarding creativity. The reason may be that as the majority of the learners belonged to the low income group, they could not afford to buy the raw materials for making creative articles as it was little expensive for them to make samples and also as they had to pay for transportation as they came by autorickshaw or by bus. They might have wished to generate income by making creative articles but they may not have had the skills to make such fine articles, which could be sold in the market, as a lot of practice is required, and knowledge about marketing for self-employment is a must. Hence, the instructors must keep in mind:

- The product should be of low cost.
- The product, which is in demand, should be produced.
- The instructors should develop skills of adult learners for making creative articles.
- The knowledge about marketing strategies should also be provided.

Pillai (2001) also reported that income-generating programmes are the most desired ones. Low cost and no cost materials should be tried out. Articles which are in demand should be produced and sold at rates lower than the market rates, keeping the quality intact. It was also found that the adult learners had a very high opinion regarding the instructors. The reason could be many. One reason could be that a lot of planning and pre-preparation were done on the part of instructors to conduct the Adult Education Programme. The instructors must have done rehearsals to conduct the adult education programme.

The instructors might have studied the psychology and characteristics of adults. They have knowledge regarding how to deal with the adults in different situations. Vir (2000) also reported that the most important skill required by the instructors is to understand adult psychology and principles of adult learning. Teaching an adult is entirely different from teaching a child, because adult is an experienced person who has already gone through various phases of life. Therefore, the psychology and method of teaching an adult differ from those employed in teaching a child. It might also be possible that, as the instructors were the students of final year (B.Sc.), they were getting trained under teacher supervisors to conduct the adult education programme. Hence, they might have given good performance, as they wanted to show their capabilities, talents and potentials and earn good grades. Shukla (1985) also found that instructors gave a good performance. They used a clear and loud voice, took personal interest in women learners. They went to women personally and spoke to them in a pleasant and soft voice, and shared a good rapport with the learners.

Further, it was found that majority of the adult learners had high opinion regarding the "physical aspect" of the programme as it was very well planned and maintained a laboratory where all the required facilities are available like gas, wash basin, utensils, comfortable chairs, desks, light, fans, etc. Another reason could be that the available facilities had made the adult learners comfortable in the environment where they saw many new faces and learnt many new things. Similar findings were reported by Omoruyi (2001), that if the timing, the duration of the classes and the pattern of teaching were satisfactory it attracted more learners. Dangi (2002) also found that the physical facilities available at the adult education centre had a positive influence on the attendance of adults. More learners were attracted if adequate facilities included light arrangement, seating arrangement, location and timing of the centre were appropriate. It was found that the adult learners had high opinion regarding the "methods and materials" aspect of the programme. The reason may be that the teaching materials were very effective in catching attention, which may have helped the adult learners in clarifying the concepts. Teaching materials may also have motivated the adult learners by arousing the curiosity of the learners. It might also be possible that the pace of slow learners might have increased with the help of teaching materials used in the adult education programme as a person can easily gain and recall the knowledge with the help of images, pictures, diagrams and different audio-visual aids.

Singh (2001) also reported that enlarged supply of teaching aids, specially printed material, radio and television can spread the message more effectively, quickly and accurately. There is a need to pay more attention to creating good educational software for both print and electronic media. Hence, the maximum number of teaching aids should be used by the instructors, which should be attractive and able to catch attention, appropriate to the content and should also have images, pictures or diagrams which would help the adult learners to sharpen their memory.

Ghosh and Sikdar (2000) found that to overcome the problems of slow learners, the following factors were found to be influencing

- proper methodology of teaching.
- well equipped teaching materials
- proper use of mass media.

Further, the findings revealed that discussion and demonstration was found to be the most effective method. The reason may be that through the discussion method the aduit ieamers may have developed their ability to discuss which might have increased the self-confidence in them to share their experiences and facts. It might also be possible that through the discussion method the adult learners were able to bring out all the different point of views to solve a problem, which might have also enhanced their critical thinking. Hence, more number of discussions can be held by the instructors for the adult learners. While conducting the discussion the instructors should make the learners feel free to discuss their ideas and they should get acquainted with the whole group as well as the instructors. It should also be kept in mind by the instructors that importance should be given to the views of the adult learners so that they feel motivated to participate in the discussion. However, in the case of demonstration method the adult learners were able to see and understand each step before proceeding to the next step. Hence, the clear view might have resulted into the clear understanding on the part of adult learners.

Shukla (1985) also found in her study that demonstration were found to be more effective than the workshop method. While conducting the workshop, sometime classroom management becomes difficult if the group becomes disorganised in their way of working and not much topic can be covered through the workshop method. It also demands a lot of time from participants and instructors and requires special facilities and materials.

SIGNIFICANT DIFFERENCES IN THE OPINION OF THE ADULT LEARNERS REGARDING THE ADULT EDUCATION PROGRAMME

The findings of the study revealed that there were no significant differences in the opinions with respect to the age, educational level, personality dimension and motivation to learn. Adult learners having age ranging from 20 years to 50 years or above were similar in their opinions regarding the adult education programme. Their age, educational qualification, personality and motivation in no way affected their opinion regarding the Adult Education Programme. The reason may be that effectiveness of adult education programme was more depended upon the teacher supervisors and instructors and their way of teaching instead of the learner's age, educational level, personality and motivation. If the instructors taught well with proper teaching aids, teaching methods, well-modulated voice, appropriate pitch, tone, they would be more appealing to the learners inspite of their different characteristics. Hence, this finding implies that for the adult education classes to be effective there should be a useful content and instructors should be well trained so that the adult learners have high opinion in future also regarding the adult education programme.

However, a significant difference was found in the opinions and regularity in attendance of the adult learners. The adult learners who were irregular had different opinion regarding the Adult Education Programme in comparison to the adults who were regular in attending. The reason may be that irregular adults may have not found the programme meaningful. The adult learners who were regular in the programme might be very enthusiastic to know 'What next'? Maybe they were acquainted with the presentation style of the programme, whereas, it might be possible that irregular adults had no idea about the manner in which the programme was conducted. When the continuity of attending the programme breaks, they may find it boring and less interesting. Hence, they were indifferent in their opinion regarding the adult education programme.

Hazarika (1971) also found that on an average women sometimes remained absent in the adult education classes. Hence, they were not able to generate interest in the activities of the Adult Education Programme. So, the value of the adult education programme should be realised by the irregular adult learners. The instructors should motivate the adult learners by making them understand the needs and the importance of the Adult Education Programme. Adult education helps the adult learners in broadening mental horizons, widens choices and increases the capacity to take decisions. Since decision decides direction and direction decides destiny, adult education enables the adult learners to take control of their destiny. Adult education helps the adult learners to acquire the ability to shape their life. It not only enables them to bring about desired changes in their own lives but also provides proper guidance to younger generation. Instructors should also make the adult learners realise that today women's education can be regarded as important as that of males. It has rightly been said, "If you educate a boy, you educate an individual but if you educate a girl, you educate a family."

Reasons for Not Attending the Adult Education Classes

It was found that a majority of the adult learners had no reason for not attending the adult education programme as a majority of them were regular. However, some of the adult learners stated that they were not aware about the place where the classes were conducted. The reason may be that the publicity for the programme may not have been done properly. Or they knew the Home Science Faculty but did not know where exactly the 'Pragati Centre' was located. It might also be possible that they had enquired from the girls of Home Science who did not know that the adult education classes were conducted in the Department of Home Science Extension and Communication as they may be from some other department.

So, the teacher supervisors and instructors together should make efforts to plan and implement the publicity of the programme effectively. Indicators should also be provided inside and outside the Home Science Faculty, which shows the way to 'Pragati Centre'. This is to have a clarity and no confusion on the part of adult learners about where the 'Pragati Centre' is situated in the Faculty of Home Science.

However, some of the adult learners were not attending the adult education classes because it was expensive for them to come to 'Pragati Centre'. The reason may be that because of the long distance they had to undertake many responsibilities relating to household work. Nask (1979) also found that adult learners left the adult education classes because of family circumstances.

This finding implies that before conducting the adult education classes the instructors should study the problems of adult learners attending the adult education classes and should also find out the solutions to overcome these hurdles specially in the area of time, health and personal problems.

However, a very less percentage of the adult learners had reported that it was the time when their husband and children came home, as a majority of the adult learners were young and unmarried girls.

Suggestions

The following are the suggestions given by the adult learners, Urban Basic Service/ Urban Community Development Projects Community volunteers and teacher supervisors.

Suggestions Given by the Adult Learners

A majority of the adult learners suggested that computer education should be provided which shows that how enthusiastic the adult learners were to learn the computer. The reason may be that they could not afford to pay fees to learn computers, whereas, in 'Pragati Centre' they could get free computer education. Another reason could be that in today's world computer education is in demand. The adult learners might have felt inferior and handicapped when they met others who knew computers. Hence, the basic computer education classes for the adult learners at no cost or low cost was suggested.

Further, a majority of the adult learners suggested that more opportunities should be provided for self-expression. The reason may be that everybody needs to express their self, to communicate clearly with others. The adult learners may also want others to listen to them. Opportunities for self-expression may also motivate them to share their experiences and discuss their problems freely so that they can also get the solutions at the same time from different people and listen to different points of view. Further, it was suggested by a majority of the adult learners that library facility should be provided. The reason may be that they wanted to increase their knowledge and build a reading habit. As they had a low educational level, they may not have got the opportunity to continue their education but they may have a strong wish to learn more. It may also be possible that they wanted to engage themselves in reading so that family members did not feel that they were free and they did not have any work to do. Hence, this finding implies that a better learning environment can be created if the library facility is provided which would help the adult learners to continue their education, develop reading habit and make them well informed. Sharma and Khandai (2001) also suggested that library facility and reading room should be provided to create a learning environment for the adult learners and also for creating a learning society. Further, the adult learners suggested that prior information should be provided before starting the Adult Education Programme regarding the place where the classes are to be conducted, class timing, who are the instructors, the activities to be conducted in the programme, duration of the programme, etc. That means advertisement or publicity should be done very effectively, neither too early nor too late, and a reminder should also be given to the adult learners about the programme so that the adult learners can be motivated to attend the programme.

It was also suggested that charts and posters through which instructors taught should be used more, and the contents should be written and displayed along with them. The reason may be they could read on their own at their own pace and follow instructions easily. It might also help them to recall the contents taught to them. Adult learners further suggested that most topics should be taught through drama. It might be that it was easy to understand the contents when they were dramatised as it allowed better concentration on the content rather than when it was presented in the form of a lecture or talk.

Rani and Eswaraiah (2002) also found that a majority of the learners were interested only in recreational programme instead of other informative and educative programme, which were necessary for the welfare of individuals and social development. Hence, this finding implies that possible messages should be imparted to the adult learners through dramas so that both informative as well as recreational aim could be achieved. Adult learners also suggested that written information should be provided in the form of booklets. The reason may be that many things were going on in their mind because of which they were not be able to remember the content after the class. Or their memories were not very sharp or they wished to keep booklets for their future reference. It was also suggested that Adult Education Programmes should be conducted in the community where they lived. The reason may be that it would be convenient for them as they would not have to pay for the transportation and also nobody would have opposition to joining the Adult Education Programme when it was conducted in the community itself. However, the disadvantage in this following suggestion is that instructors would not be able to use a variety of media through which they could convey the message effectively. Sometimes facilities like electricity may not be available in the community hall. Hence, it may be difficult for the instructors to conduct the programme effectively in the community.

Lastly, it was suggested that certificates should be provided to them so that they could have a proof that they had attended the literacy classes. It could act as incentive and also motivate the adult learners to attend the classes regularly.

Suggestions Given by the UBS/UCD Community Volunteers

Thoughtful attention should be given to the needs of the learners, openness, which eases the expression of views and professional guidance, should be ensured these points were suggested by the majority of the UBS/UCD Community volunteers. The reasons for these suggestions may be that learners would take interest in the programme if it were based on their needs and interests. First their needs should be satisfied and their problem should be solved, then the instructors should proceed with the actual programme of delivery, which they feel is important.

Singh (2001) reported that a successful educational system is that which is able to create awareness among clients and unite them to solve their problems collectively. For that, instructors should identify the needs of the learners and plan the programme accordingly. If the programme is based on their interests, they will be motivated to participate in the programme and will naturally express their views.

Sharma and Patel (1986) reported that programmes must be built on basic needs (expressed or unexpressed), immediate and felt problems and interests of the concerned people and their community. 'Professional guidance' should be provided, was suggested by many. The reason could be that the adult learners may have different abilities and hidden talents, which could be enhanced and utilised if proper guidance is provided to them.

It was also suggested by Sharma and Patel (1986) that emphasis should be laid on vocationalisation related to the local environment. The aim of this programme should not only to be to impart education to illiterate adults but also to improve the community life. The gap between the world of letter and world of work should be narrowed.

Gireesan (2000) also suggested that necessary technical guidance and expertise should be solicited from technical training institutions for organising vocation-oriented courses for the benefit of the learners. Other suggestions given by the UBS/ UCD Community volunteers were that the programme should be conducted regularly, i.e., for the whole year. The reason may be that a large number of communities can be covered within a year whereas, the Adult Education Programme is conducted for four months only. As a result the majority of the women who are from the weaker section of the society can get the benefit of this programme. It was also suggested that the whole area, i.e., Fatehgunj, where the Home Science Faculty in which the programme is conducted is located, should be covered by the Adult Education Programme. Those who are dropouts and from the weaker section of the society should not be left out. Further, it was suggested that the programme should be conducted in the slum community instead of the Faculty of Home Science, as it would be more convenient for the beneficiaries to attend the classes. Reason for such a suggestion may be that they were thinking form their point of view and in terms of their convenience.

Suggestions Given by the Teacher Supervisor

Teacher supervisors suggested that awareness regarding marketing strategies should be provided to sell the products. The reason may be that the adult learners had put in so much effort to make the product but their efforts could be utilised only if the knowledge regarding marketing is also provided. As Jhansi and Misra (2000) reported, a major chunk of the youth population is unable to find employment due to various reasons, including literacy, faulty educational training, low wages and over population. Adult learners thus require vocational training and technical education, which, in turn, will prepare them to get gainful employments. This mode of education can be covered within the gamut of adult literacy programmes. So, it can be said that by providing the vocational training the adult learners can generate income, which may give them the feeling of satisfaction, the motivation to learn further and they will also participate interestingly in the adult education programme.

As Suguna (2001) reported, participation has two dimensions—quantitative and qualitative. People's participation in terms of numbers has no meaning. Today there is a need for change from quantitative to qualitative. Hence, this finding implies that if the knowledge of marketing strategies will be provided to them, their quantitative participation can be change in the qualitative participation in the programme. Further, suggestions given by the teacher supervisors were inclusion of ice breaking session should be arranged for the adult learners in the very beginning of the programme to help the target group to open up easily with the instructors and make them feel comfortable at the same time in the adult education programme. Further, it was suggested that product demonstration should be market-oriented, it should have some value in the market or it should be demanded by the customers so that it can be sold in the market.

More of "need felt" topics should be incorporated, e.g., environment, energy health, etc. It was also suggested that message should be imparted through games. The reason may be that more number of games would make the programme interesting and also it would be easy for the adult learners to learn. Games like puzzles, quizzes, one minute, etc., should be included not only for recreation but for conveying the message effectively, as games can break the monotony and can encourage participation of adult learners.

Further, it was suggested that exhibition should be made a permanent feature of the programme. This could be because the environment influences a person. A person will react according to the environment in which he/she is. Hence, through the exhibition learning environment can be created in which adult learners can be encouraged and motivated to learn.

Kumar, Singh and Singh (2000) had suggested in their study that there is a need to create an environment for ensuring motivation of the target groups and voluntary workers so as to carry forward the literacy campaigns to phase of continuing education programme. Hence, this finding implies that a good learning environment should be created for the adult learners with the help of charts, posters, flashcards, flipcharts, mobiles, specimens, models, booklet, etc., which can attract the attention of the adult learners so that they can concentrate in the adult education programme without diverting their minds in other matters of life. On the basis of the above discussion, it can be concluded that the younger adult learners had a low educational level but they were extroverts and in spite of having low motivation they were regular in the class. They were very enthusiastic and expressive which promoted active participation in the Adult Education Programme. The result of present study shows that overall the adult learners had high opinion regarding the programme implying a favourable attitude and a willingness to learn as the programme was well planned and executed by the instructors and teacher supervisors which resulted in an effective adult programme.

Instructors gave good performance and put all their efforts to make the programme effective and meaningful. Physical facilities available at the 'Pragati Centre' had a positive influence on the adult learners in attending the programme. Adult learners also had high opinion regarding the curriculum of the programme but still there is a scope to give more attention towards the curriculum. Teaching materials were very effective in catching attention, which have helped the adult learners in clarifying the concepts. However, significant differences were found with regard to regularity in attendance of the adult learners. Those who were regular had a high opinion in comparison to those who were irregular.

Lastly, it can be concluded that the value and the importance of adult education programme should be realised by the irregular adult learners so that they can cope up with the demand of living and working. The facilities like transportation, computer education, library child care centre facility, etc., if provided, could make the adult education programme more powerful.

6

Summary and Conclusion

In the learning society, colleges and universities will have a leading responsibility for providing continuous educational opportunities. Until the 1940s higher education was largely for young elite; from 1945 to 1970, the pattern began to shift toward mass higher learning, although one which was still primarily youth-oriented. In the future, though, there will be strong moves to universal access to higher education for all adults, making available the resources of institutions to virtually all elements of society. In everyday life, however, the expression, "adult education", is often used in another sense, as a collective term covering the institutions and procedures by which adults are enabled and encouraged to experience the process. For many people, this mechanism is adult education.

> Adult education is the action of an external educational agent in purposefully ordering behavior into planned systematic experiences that can result in learning for those for whom such activity is supplemental to their primary role in society, and which involves some continuity in an exchange relationship between the agent and the learner so that the educational process is under constant supervision and direction.

The multidisciplinary nature of the field and its practitioners create many problems in international communication. It is only recently that the concept of adult education as a discrete sector of education has been recognised in many countries; even today some societies view the education and training of their citizens from the perspective of the function such training performance or the class to which participants belong; for example, trade union education or working class education. The term, "adult education", denotes the entire body of organised educational processes, whatever the content, level, and method, whether formal or otherwise, or whether they prolong or replace initial education in schools, colleges, and universities, as well as an apprenticeship, where by persons regarded as adult by the society to which they belong develop their abilities, enrich their knowledge, improve their technical or professional qualifications, or turn them in a new direction and bring about changes in their attitudes or behaviour in the twofold perspective of full personal development and participation in balanced and independent social, economic and cultural development.

Many concepts closely related to adult education, used in the literature since the early 1960s, continue to be subject to controversy. These include "formal", "non-formal", "informal", "lifelong learning", "lifelong education", "continuing education" and "recent education".

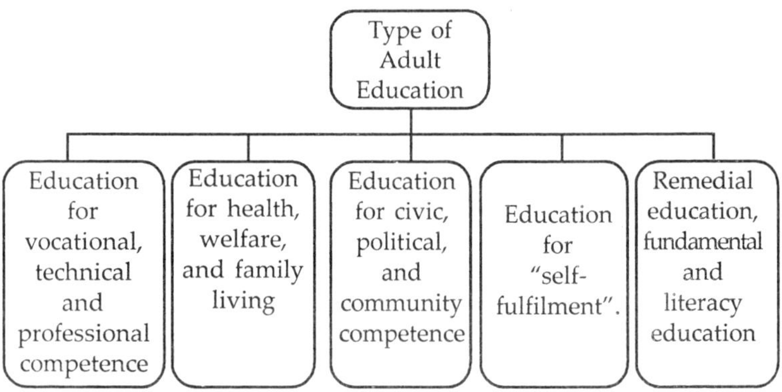

The term "adult education" has come into general use within the last half century to identify two different but related phenomena: a field of social activity and an emerging discipline in social science. Although different, these phenomena are interdependent. The discipline finds its subject of study in the field, which is, in turn, dependent upon the discipline for its development. It may be mentioned that in India adult education has travelled a long way, at least in programme implementation. In the early fifties it was known as the 'Social Education' programme. Then came a change in the areas of emphasis and the contents of the programme were given a slant. The changed programme came to be known as 'Fundamental Education', as citizenship education in a nascent democracy became of prime importance. Adult education is an impelling need, the need is so imperative and over-powering that all men and women must be helped to acquire the skills and knowledge that would enable them to properly fit into the society which is fast moving. Adult Education Programme as envisaged in the National Adult Education Programme is meant primarily for women and learners belonging to deprived section of the population. This does not mean that others willing to join Adult Education Programme should be excluded, but emphasis must be given to this section of the population for they constitute about 60 to 70 per cent of India's population which did not have the benefit of any type of education formal or informal.

'Pragati Centre' was started in 1983 for conducting the adult education programme in the Department of Home Science Extension and Communication. 'Pragati' is the path towards the building of women's skills shaping their thought and encouraging new ideas. It also brightens the light of awareness among the women on different issues. It helps in the professional development of the third-year students by providing the training to plan, organise and conduct the adult education programme.

In order to conduct the adult education programme, the Department of Home Science Extension and Communication had decided to contact Urban Basic Service (UBS) and Urban Community Development (UCD) Community volunteers to bring the adult learners to the Department of Home Science Extension and Communication. Much of the success of the Adult Education Programme will depend upon the manner in which it is implemented and evaluated. The aim of evaluating the Adult Education Programme of 'Pragati Centre' is not to 'prove' but to 'improve' the programme. In order to be suitable and effective the Adult Education Programme needs to be evaluated from time to time.

So, the investigator had undertaken a study of an appraisal of Adult Education Programme of 'Pragati Centre' of the Department of Home Science Extension and Communication.

Statement of the Problem

Looking at the above scenario of adult education programme it was decided to take up a study on "An appraisal of Adult Education Programme of 'Pragati Centre' of the Department of Home Science Extension and Communication, Faculty of Home Science, The M.S.University, Baroda in the year 2003-2004."

Objectives of the Study

1. To develop the profile of adult learners who attended the Adult Education Programme in 'Pragati Centre' of the Department of Home Science Extension and Communication.
2. To study the overall opinions of the adult learners regarding the Adult Education Programme of 'Pragati Centre' of the Department of Home Science Extension and Communication in relation to the following aspects:
    a) Curricular aspect
    b) Instructor
    c) Physical aspect
    d) Methods and materials
3. To study the overall differences in the opinions of the adult learners regarding the Adult Education Programme of 'Pragati Centre' of the Department of Extension and Communication in relation to their:
    a) Age
    b) Educational level
    c) Regularity in attendance
    d) Personality Dimension
    e) Motivation to learn
4. To find out the reasons given by the adult learners for not attending the Adult Education Programme of 'Pragati Centre' of the Department of Home Science Extension and Communication.

5. To obtain suggestions regarding the improvement of the Adult Education Programme of 'Pragati Centre' of the Department of Home Science Extension and Communication from the:
   a) Adult learners
   b) UBS/UCD community volunteers
   c) Teacher Supervisors

Assumptions of the Study

1. Adult learners have some opinions regarding the Adult Education Programme of 'Pragati Centre' of the Department of Home Science Extension and Communication.
2. Adult learners have some reasons for not attending the Adult Education Programme of 'Pragati Centre of the Department of Home Science Extension and Communication.

Null Hypotheses of the Study

1. There will be no significant difference in the overall opinions of the adult learners regarding the Adult Education Programme of 'Pragati Centre' of the Department of Home Science Extension and Communication in relation to the following variables:
   a) Age
   b) Educational level
   c) Regularity in attendance
   d) Personality Dimension
   e) Motivation to learn

Delimitations of the Study

The study is delimited to the Adult Education Programme conducted in 'Pragati Centre' of the Department of Home Science Extension and Communication in the year 2003.

The study is delimited to the adults who have attended the Adult Education Programme in 'Pragati Centre' of the Department of Home Science Extension and Communication.

Description of the Population

The population of the study consisted of the adult learners who attended the Adult Education Programme of 'Pragati Centre' of the Department of Home Science Extension and Communication, Faculty of Home Science in the year 2003, UBS/UCD Community Volunteers and teacher supervisors of Adult Education Programme.

Selection of the Sample

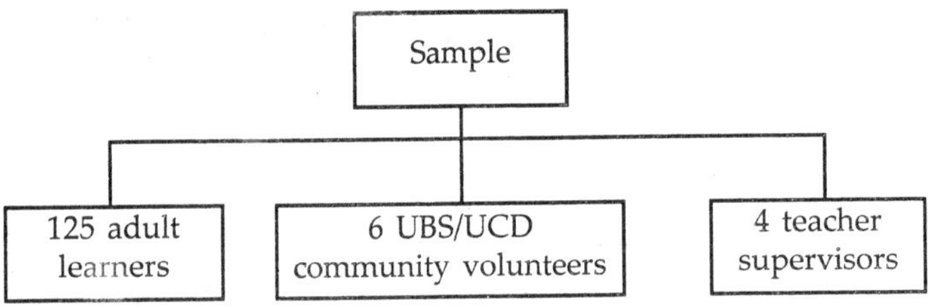

Construction of the Research Tool

A structured questionnaire was developed by the investigator. The investigator constructed the tool after reviewing related literature from journals, articles, reports, books and dissertations.

Table 1: Construction of the Tool and the Response System

Sr.No.	*Section*	*Aspects*	*Responsesystem*
1.	Profile of the adult learner	– Age	Checklist
		– Educational level	Checklist
		– Regularity in attendance	Checklist
		– Personality	2 point scale
		– Motivation to learn	4 point scale
2.	Opinions of the adult learners	– Curriculum aspect – Instructor	3 point scale and open ended.

(Contd...)

(Contd...)

		– Physical aspect – Methods and materials	
3.	Reasons for not attending the classes	–	2 point scale
4.	Suggestions	– Adult learners – UBS/UCD community volunteers – Teacher Supervisors	3 point scale and open ended.

Validation of the Tool

To check the content and construct validity the tool was given to seven different experts. Out of these, six experts were from the Faculty of Home Science and one expert from the Faculty of Education and Psychology, The M.S.University Baroda, Vadodara.

Collection of Data

Data collection was done in the months of December and January 2004. The investigator used home visit method to collect the data from the adult learners and personally contacted UBS/UCD Community volunteers and teacher supervisors in their respective offices.

Plan for Statistical Analysis

Statistical Measures for the Analysis of the Data

Sr.No.	*Purpose*	*Statistical measures*
1.	Background information of the respondents.	Percentage
2.	Overall opinions reported by the adult learners.	Percentage

(Contd...)

(Contd...)

3.	Overall opinion reported by adult learnersaccording to the variables.	Percentage
4.	Item wise opinions reported by the adult learners.	Intensity Indices
5.	Overall Differences in the opinions according to thevariables.	Chi-Square
6.	Reasons for not attending the adult education classes.	Percentage
7.	Suggestions from:	
	– Adult learners	Percentage
	– Teacher SupervisorsPercentage	
	– UBS/UCD Community Volunteers.	Percentage

Major Findings

Background Information of the Respondents

A majority of the adult learners were young, i.e., below 25 or 25 years of age. They had a low educational level and they were regular in attending the classes. A majority of these were by nature extroverts but had low motivation to learn. It was found that majority of the adult learners were Hindus, living in joint families and belonging to the low-income group. When marital status was checked, it was found that a majority of the adult learners were unmarried and not employed as they had low educational level.

Opinions of the Adult Learners Regarding the Adult Education Programme

- Overall a majority of the respondents had a high opinion regarding the Adult Education Programme. Only 22 two per cent of them had a moderaie opinion and nobody had a low opinion of the programme.
- Percentage-wise, in all the categories of variables except regularity in attendance, the respondents had almost equal percentage of high and moderate opinion regarding the Adult Education Programme. On the other hand those who were regular had a high opinion in comparison to those who were irregular.

- Aspect-wise, majority of the adult learners had high opinion regarding the physical aspects, instructors, methods and materials, curricular aspect respectively.
- The adult learners had opined that the Adult Education Programme provided the knowledge, which was useful in day-to-day life and helped in increasing the literacy level of the learners. This finding shows that the adult learners got benefit through the adult education programme in terms of increase in knowledge.
- The adult learners were concerned for their self-development to a moderate level which is a very positive sign of development, considering that they had low education, low income and came from poor families.
- The findings of the "health aspect" of the programme revealed that the adult learners were concerned to a great extent to find out about new recipes, try out new recipes and also keep a check on their nutritive value and monitor diets of their family members.
- The adult learners had moderate opinion regarding creativity aspect of the programme as majority of them belonged to the low-income group so they could not afford to buy the raw materials for making creative articles.
- A majority of the adult learners opined that instructors were punctual in the class, they were helping and caring, their language was clearly understood and they were confident while conducting the classes.
- It was also found that majority of the adult learners had a high opinion regarding the "physical aspect" of the programme as it was very well planned and maintained laboratory where all the required facilities are available like gas, wash basin, utensils, comfortable chairs, desks, light, fans etc. which had a positive influence on the attendance of adult learners.
- A majority of the adult learners opined that several teaching aids were used which were well prepared. It was also found that specimens and posters were most effective teaching aids and discussion and demonstrations were found to be the most effective teaching methods in clarifying the concepts to the adult learners.

- No significant differences were found in opinions regarding the Adult Education Programme according to age, educational level, personality dimension and motivation to learn.
- Significant differences were found in opinions regarding the Adult Education Programme according to regularity in attendance.

Reasons for Not Attending the Adult Education Classes

- The location of the classes was not known and it was expensive to come to 'Pragati Centre' because of its long distance from their home, found to be the major reasons for not attending the adult education classes.

Suggestions Obtained from Adult Learners, UBS/UCD Community Volunteers and Teacher Supervisors

- Computer education and more opportunities for self-expression were suggested by the majority of the adult learners.
- It was suggested that 'professional guidance' should be provided in which emphasis should be given on vocationalisation related to the local environment so that different abilities of the adult learners could be enhanced and utilised.
- Awareness regarding marketing strategies to sell the products should be created was suggested by the majority of the teacher supervisors. Adult learners made so many efforts to make the product but their efforts could be utilised only if the knowledge regarding marketing was also provided.
- It was also suggested that product demonstration should be market oriented. It should have some value in the market and it should be demanded by the customers so that it can be sold in the market.
- Education should be imparted through games and dramatic methods as more number of games and dramas will make the programme interesting and would help the adult learners to learn easily.

The aim of this study was to evaluate the adult education programme by studying the opinions of the adult learners and checking carefully the different aspect of the programme of 'Pragati Centre', which was essential for bringing about improvements in the quality of the Adult Education Programme of 'Pragati Centre'. This study indicated that the adult learners gained from the Adult Education Programme but certain aspects needed to be strengthened like education, self-development, health and creativity aspect of the programme. However, the adult learners had overall high opinion regarding the education programme. They found that the instructors were helping, friendly and confident while conducting the classes. They used appropriate methods and materials, which helped them to gain and recall the knowledge more easily. The instructors were advised to use more number of drama and game methods for imparting education. Physical facilities were adequate and had made the adult learners feel comfortable in the 'Pragati Centre'.

This study also emphasised that everyone in a learning society has to be literate. To justify any society being called a meaningful and good learning society, the adult learners should realise how important the Adult Education Programme is in removing the innumerable hurdles from a person's life as it is tool of learning an instrument of social change. Women prefer programmes, which are entertaining, economically beneficial and have immediate use. If such points are considered, adult education programme will go a long way in the path of success. Sincere involvement and deeper interest on the part of teacher supervisors and instructors will also help in the improvement and the success of the programme.

Adult education centres should be set up in planned manner in order to supplement the efforts of the formal system. The time, place and curriculum of the NFE should be convenient and relevant to the needs, conditions and interests of the learners. Voluntary and private agencies should be encouraged to shape the responsibilities in providing adult education centres. Local communities such as professional bodies should be made direct responsible for such education. Gram panchayats, Lion's Clubs. Direct links between formal and non-formal system should be established and nobody should have any difficulty in switching over one to the other. Cheap, innovative learning materials need to be developed for various groups suiting the needs and interests of learners and it should be easily available. Methods and media suitable for the learners in different age-groups and with various socio-cultural background should be adopted and utilised for the teaching-learning process. Proper evaluation procedures should be developed and practised for ascertaining the progress, placement and certification of the learners.

The ailments mentioned above are hindering the way of adult education. Unfortunately, there is no clear-cut solution. These problems are certainly of many shades of gray, the success of the Adult Education Programme can be met if instruments derived from modern technology, with its limitless possibilities are put to use on an adequate scale and with appropriate means. The educational policies should not be laid down from above but the policy decisions must be made at the local level and that too with the participation of people. Literacy programmes should be provided only for well motivated adults. Ivan Iliich has demonstrated that well motivated adults make as much progress in a year as might be accomplished by the children in six years of elementary school. We need to learn from the best of our research, theory and practice and then boldly struggle to make adult education a success. The quality of training and functionaries is poor, even the monitoring and evaluation system lacks credibility there is considerable misreporting. Mass media do not provide any support we hardly read success stories in newspaper. Voluntary agencies do not receive cooperation from state governments and the procedures for their involvement discourage them. Achievement of literacy level generally is below the expectation and the components of functionality remain neglected. Absence of post-literacy and continuing education achievements adversely affect the programme. Political and administrative support of the state governments and panchayati raj institutions is not forthcoming in a sustained manner.

Nationwide Work Strategy

– *Increase motivation:* The central issue in literacy is motivation. The whole nation has been designed to face this issue. The increase in motivation can be done by various ways such as secure people's participation. People's participation can be done through media and communication, creation of local level participatory structures, taking out of *jatthaas*, training of cadres of youth etc.

- *Significantly increase involvement of voluntary agencies:* Diverse methods can be used for identification of suitable voluntary organisations, procedures of financial assistance and voluntary agencies involved on a massive scale for spread of the programmes, for training and technical resource development experimentation, innovation, etc.
- *Substantially improve ongoing programme:* The programme quality must be improved substantially by application of sciences and technology inputs, better supervision, suitable training, pedagogical innovations, etc.
- *Mass movement*: This must be launched for literacy involving educational institutions, teachers, students, youths, military and parliamentary personnel, housewives, ex-servicemen, employers, trade unions, etc.
- *Ensure availability of standard learning material:* The structure of technical resource development at the national, state as well as district levels must ensure material of good quality, and conforming to the objectives of NLM.
- Regular programmes on radio and television for information, motivation and active involvement should be telecasted.
- Newspapers can be used systematically for creating a positive attitude towards promotion of literacy among the influential section of society.
- Village education committee can be formed and Jatthas-cultural caravans be used for new education.

The university's responsibilities in lifelong learning include providing access to programmes for students outside the full-time, residential pattern and also providing the inculcation of values and the development of skills in continuous learning for all students. Lifelong learning opportunities are needed in all phases of knowledge and professions, and should be made available to serve the educational interests and changing careers of college graduates as well as those without degrees who want to gain new skills and lead more productive lives.

As important as the functions of the university are the campus is not the only location for continuous education. New technology and the sheer volume of agencies and institutions supplying educational opportunities make it potentially possible for education of high quality to be universally available. The newest knowledge and the best teachers can be brought into factories and homes and into the most isolated communities through the use of television; indeed, every home can be a classroom. In cooperation with other institutions, the university should make educational opportunities available for all citizens everywhere.

Many adults are independent learners and they can be attracted to continue their education by the adaption of teaching and learning to their circumstances. Universities should lead in research on the independent learner and independent learning. Research on what motivates adults to learn and which material can teach a subject best should result in an expansion of educational opportunities to assist independent learning. Few educators believe that only full-time study can be serious and the only environments within which adults can learn. Changing educational needs should be taken account of and strong efforts should be made to improve access to programmes. It is obvious in higher education that all segments operate with limited resources. In most universities, educational programmes are funded at less than optimum levels. Much research is needed, both basic and applied, and too few resources exist with which to carry out the extension work.

The general conception is that institutions of higher learning have enormous intellectual resources available to assist in providing alternative methods and approaches to solving social problems. As universities have increased in size, they have increased their involvement with government, business, organised labour and other institutions. The task of training of teachers for schools at various levels should be undertaken primarily by training schools and institutes affiliated to boards of education and state departments of education, and teacher education colleges and university departments affiliated to various universities. Teacher education colleges, as compared to general education colleges, are better suited to undertake the responsibility and task of adult and continuing education due to the following reasons:

1) Education colleges deal with the methodology of teaching children and have the basic infrastructure for evolving methods and materials for adults learning.
2) The pupil teachers undertake supervised teaching in schools. This dimension of their work can be extended to teaching adult literacy classes.
3) Pupil teachers form more or less a lot committed to the profession of teaching. Hence, they are likely to possess attitudes more conducive to the work of teaching adults than these of general education colleges.
4) The curriculum, personnel and practices followed in education colleges can be easily adapted to the requirement of adult education.
5) The pupil teachers possess a bachelor's degree as a minimum qualification for entry into colleges and many of them possess master's degrees. Hence, they are better off than their counterparts in undergraduate classes in terms of knowledge of content and self-confidence required in a teacher.

The emergence of new area of working with community has provided an opportunity to education colleges to participate in the work of community development through adult and continuing education. Universities are the creation of the society and serve the community of which they are part. Educational systems cannot now afford to remain a closed circuit. The non-formal nature of continuing education makes it easier to absorb the new NAEP-National Adult Education Progamme. Continuing education is a process of achieving integration of knowledge with life or as a process of rectifying the imbalance created by formal education in individual as well as community life.

At the undergraduate level students may be involved for undertaking literacy classes in two phases: one phase will consist of 10 to 12 weeks period for running the adult education centres regularly, and this could be possible either in the vacations or it should be adjusted with the theory classes. In the second phase, which will again consist of 10 to 12 weeks but the students may go to make contact at these centres at the weekend. Each student should be allotted five to ten families of a village/mohalla /or ward where the number of illiterates is around 10 in number. A student should be declared 'pass,' unless his practical or extension work is not completed. Most of the universities are situated in urban areas, and therefore adult education centres for them may be urban centres. Similarly, each student should be asked to take up post-literacy and follow-up work with the families already allotted to them in the third phase of the programme in the next year. At the postgraduate level, the students should be asked to carry out extension work by taking up a project or dissertation where they should be required to devote their time for this work for not less than six months. It should generally be for a period from 6 to 10 months. Their result should not be declared unless they complete this part of their curriculum.

One innovation of particular importance to the field would be the inclusion of an adult education component in school teacher-training courses. At present very few institutions of teacher training pay any more than lip service to the notion of lifelong learning. If schools are to become centres of lifelong learning then their staff will need a greater understanding of adult psychology and practice in teaching adult students. Teacher-training courses could widen their curriculum to include such a component. It has also been suggested that school governing bodies and management boards should include an adult education representation. Given that crucial decisions concerning school operations and priorities rest in the hands of such bodies, adult educators will continue to experience a sense of marginality and vulnerability if their interests remain unrepresented. Schools are, after all, the agencies of education provision into which is poured the greater part of governmental educational expenditure. They are accessible sites of educational activity located in many villages, all towns, and urban neighborhoods. If the adults of tomorrows are to be lifelong learners possessing self-directed learning skills and the ability to adapt to periods of retraining at various times during their working lives, then it is the schools which will be responsible for developing the required cognitive skills and affective dispositions. Many programmes place complete faith in the country's youth teachers and workers and peasants. In conformity with that spirit, it is intended to give a marked slant to programmes from the present intensive selective activity on a limited scale to a mass programme.

1. Literacy work would be taken up by a large number of students as "study service", viz., specific projects taken up as a part of work experience and social/national service.
2. Substantial institutional incentive will be provided to universities, colleges, schools for eradication of literacy.

Individuals should be encouragged to look upon literacy work as personal commitment and voluntary services, particularly by women among women, and involvement of voluntary agencies. It is recognised that literacy is as much a basic need for education is the basic need for human development and human development is the basic need for economic development. Economic development does not automatically increases the quantity or quality of human development. Human development is now considered an important input in eradication of poverty. However we have learned over the years that the meaning of literacy and education evolve. The *Webster Dictionary* defines education as the process of educating or teaching. Educating is further defined as to develop the "knowledge, skill, or character of..."Thus from these definitions we might assume that the purpose of education is to develop the knowledge, skill or character of student. When we drill down to the purpose of 'Education for what', we start to see many different definitions cultural literacy, functional literacy, basic literacy, neo-literacy, primary education, skill training, etc. Let us, for example, consider the age factor education for children, age 0-3(pre-school), 6-140(typically forcing on children who should be in school but are not due to various factors) all perhaps fall under the educational bracket.

The importance of post-literacy and continuing education programmes has now been universally recognised but these programmes generally are not undertaken systematically and with as much care as desired. By and large the post-literacy programmes are organised after the literacy drives are over and many a time after a long gap. This results illiteracy, and neo-literates are left to live in ignorance and cultural deprivation. The situation has to be changed. In fact, the post-literacy and continuing education programmes should be undertaken before literacy campaigns are started. This will create a favourable atmosphere for learning and would create motivation even among the non-literates to learn and acquire literacy skills.

The post-literacy and continuing education programmes should aim at reinforcement and stabilisation of literacy skills; enhancement of the comprehension and understanding of the subjects taught as part of general education;- opening new avenues for learning vocational and social skills necessary for social and economic betterment and reinforcement, and acceleration of the process of conscientisation for securing rightful place in the socio-economic order and for sharing the benefits and opportunities made available by the advancement of science and technology.

The scheme of Jan Shikshan Nilayam (JSN) in the NLM was conceptually very sound. It was the first attempt to institutionalise adult education. But it had some basic deficiencies which proved to be bottlenecks in achieving the desired results. The multifarious activities of a JSNs were difficult to be achieved by a part time *prerak* of Rs.200 p.m. There was no proper place for the Nilayam. Had we provided permanent and sufficient space for the Nilayam and have appointed a full time *prerak*, the results would have been different?

The recent proposal of the Government of India to start Continuing Education Centres (CECs) in every village is welcome. It will solve some of the pitfalls of JSNs. But many still remain unsolved. The *prerak* again is a part-time person with a poor honorarium. The budget both recurring and non recurring is again on a low side which will not be sufficient to carry out the multifarious activities of a CEC. It is a better to have a relook at the entire scheme of CEC so that it does not meet the fate of JSNs. Before the scheme is implemented it is necessary to organise zonal seminars to discuss the scheme in which representative of governmental, non-governmental organisations and universities should be invited. The scheme should be launched on the basis of the recommendations of the zonal seminars. The proper functioning of the Continuing Education Centre will be an important step in achieving the cherished goal of a learning society.

The Ghosh Committee recommendation to add two rooms to any existing public building in a village—one for a library and the other for continuing education—is a very important suggestion and should be implemented without delay. The permanent and sufficient space for a CEC will definitely make it a functional centre. In places where CECs are not started, it as essential to start a village library. The libraries play an effective role in checking relapse into illiteracy. There is an unrevocable relation between literacy and the library, and for the good of both this relationship should not only be maintained but strengthened. But to keep the readers' interest alive in the library it is essential that there should be constant flow of new books to the library. The mobile library also plays a significant role in the post-literacy and continuing education. It provides the right book to the right reader at the right time, and right at the doorstep. But the books in the library should be of readers' needs and interests. Areas not covered by CEC and rural library should be covered by a mobile library.

In the strategies for post-literacy and continuing education, publication of a newsletter occupies an important place. It has the distinct advantage of stabilising knowledge of reading and writing and providing current information to the neo-literates and to the other members of the family right at the doorstep. Some PL/CE districts have started publishing newsletters. But the need is to multiply the efforts so that neo-literates get useful information for betterment of their lives. But before starting a newsletter the persons connected with the work should be properly oriented in editing and distribution so that the right message reaches the people at the right time. A number of strategies are needed for achieving the objectives of post-literacy and continuing education. The visual media can also be used for the purpose. In any programme of post-literacy and continuing education the community should be the focus. If that is done it will create the necessary motivation among the non-literates also which is very much lacking. In addition to vocational courses, the training courses in health and family welfare, national integration, nutrition, human rights and environmental education would go a long way in the social and economic progress of the country.

The panchayati raj institutions should be closely involved with post-literacy and continuing education work. They can also fruitfully link literacy and post-literacy programmes with development activities. The village panchayats should be entrusted the responsibility of starting a village library where it does not exist. Self learning opportunities will enable the people to participate effectively and meaningfully in the functioning of the panchayati raj institutions. The aim of the post-literacy programme should be to ensure the continuity both of the educational and developmental processes initiated through the literacy programme. Ultimately it should be the responsibility of the community to take over the programme so that continuity is ensured, and post-literacy and continuing education centres should become community centres in letter and spirit.

The term 'post-literacy' has come to have different meanings in various educational systems. In some countries, the term is used loosely to include all forms of education that follow after the achievement of basic literacy. In some other countries, post-literacy is defined more narrowly to simply consolidate basic literacy skills to a level equivalent to the completion of formal primary school. In this definition, post-literacy is considered as a 'bridge' between primary schooling or its equivalent and further study. The definition accepted by the National Literacy Mission lies somewhere in between these two extremes. As a part of continuing education, post-literacy programmes attempt to give interested learners an opportunity to harness and develop their learning potential after completion of a course in basic literacy. Learning skills acquired by neo-literates during the short span on the literacy campaigns are at best fragile. There is a genuine danger of neo-literates regressing into partial or total illiteracy unless special efforts are continued to consolidate, sustain and possibly enhance their literacy levels. Thus, the aim of the Mission's post-literacy programme is to consolidate the basic literacy skills of speaking, reading, writing, numeracy and problem solving, and at the same time, transform these learners into an educated 'whole person', who is a productive socio-economic asset to the community.

The National Literacy Mission has designed a one-year post-literacy programme to be implemented in a mission mode. In fact, it has laid a great deal of emphasis on the planning and launching of post-literacy programme simultaneously after conclusion of the total literacy campaigns phase. In keeping with its aims, the Mission has formulated and circulated broad guidelines for implementation of post literacy programmes. The three basic elements are:

- Identification of learning needs of neo-literates.
- Provision of learning opportunities to meet the needs.
- Creating a socio-economic, political and cultural ambience to sustain the learning environment.

Post-literacy learning strategies as developed by the National Literacy Mission envisage the provision of learning opportunities both in structured and unstructured situations. A structured situation refers to organised learning where primers or graded textual material as well as suitably designed supplementary reading books for neo-literates are used. Unstructured situations refer to widely differing literacy abilities necessitating the provision of a wide range of learning materials and tools. These range from wall newspapers to book corners or libraries. Various media like radio and television are also used along with local art forms, study tours and excursions.

The post-literacy programme thus serves as an umbrella under which a host of development activities are taken up; skill development forms a major component of post-literacy; enterprising district collectors have been able to dovetail skill development within innovative development schemes. It is during the post-literacy phase that linkages with other departments, especially with health, rural development and environment, are developed. One of the most important tasks of the post-literacy is the 'mopping up' operation or remediation. Those learners who dropped out of the total literacy campaigns phase or could not achieve the prescribed norms of literacy, are enabled to achieve the required levels. The first phase of the post-literacy programme envisages 40 hours of guided learning, focusing not only on remediation, retention and consolidation of literacy skills of neo-literates but seeking to ingrain the reading habit in them so that they are able to put their literacy skills to good use in their daily life.

The next phase of the post-literacy programme provides opportunities for unstructured learning through self-directed processes. The Jan Chetna Kendras are used as an 'open window' for dissemination of information regarding ongoing development schemes. Many districts have brought out simplified booklets on development schemes for neo-literates that have helped them to make informed choices. Districts are encouraged to create a pool of literature by holding a writers' workshop and the tapping the talent of local storytellers. Thiruchirapally district of Tamil Nadu has the distinction of having virtually completed the post-literacy programme on a totally ad hoc grant. The Thiruchirapally Mavatta Arivoli lyakkam headed by the district collector ran according to schedule and has now made the transition to the continuing education phase. The Arivoli strongpoint was that it had a wide reach and adequate presence in the rural areas - a large number of village panchayat residents, most of them women, say that they owe their posts won in the 1996 panchayat elections, to their newly acquired literacy. The 2,400 village libraries, a feature of the post-literacy stage are well used. Often little more than a tin roof shed, where books are displayed like buntings on string tied to poles, the libraries are also doubling as the headquarters of women's self-help group of the area. An interesting practice initiated by the Arivoli is to have library organisers send direct reports on postcards, on the state of basic amenities in the village ranging from hand-pumps and street lights to drinking water. These missives reach the district collector and the practice has accorded the library organisers importance in the community.

Goals for the Eleventh Plan

The target for the Eleventh Plan is to achieve 85 per cent literacy by 2012. The target for male literacy is 90 per cent and for female literacy is 80 per cent.The gender gap in literacy is to be reduced to 10 per cent along with bridging of regional, social and gender disparities. The illiterates in the 35+ age-group are also expected to be covered through a computer-based self-learning system. New models of continuing education will be developed to reach a much higher level of literacy. The goals as laid down in the Approach Paper of the Planning Commission would mean that a new age-group (35+) would be added to the target. This would mean a target ot covering many million illiterates during the Eleventh Plan. In addition, there are already 124 million neo-literates whose needs for lifelong learning have to be addressed.

Revised strategy for the Eleventh Plan

The existing schemes of Total Literacy Campaign (TLC), Post-Literacy Programme (PLP) and Continuing Education Programme (CEP) have been amalgamated into a single scheme known as 'Adult Education & Skill Development'. The thrust of the programme would be on addressing the learning needs of the illiterates and neo-literates, providing them with opportunities of lifelong learning and skill development, and linking them with issues of rights, governance and livelihoods. The new programme to be launched after amalgamating the TLC, PLP and CE stages is called Lifelong Education and Awareness Programme (LEAP). The main features of the LEAP are:

1. Different types of learning packages and learning programmes to suit the needs of various categories of beneficiaries.
2. Life skills education with focus on communication skills, problem solving skills, entrepreneurial skills, etc.
3. Information window on health, rural development, environment conservation, etc.
4. Target Specific Programme particularly Equivalency Programmes to mainstream the neo-literates and others with the formal system.
5. Rural libraries with focus on neo-literates' literature.
6. Awareness programmes to discuss on issues like RTI, REGP, NRHM, HIV/AIDS etc.

Recommendations for Future Studies

On the basis of the experience and findings of the study it is felt necessary to recommend studies in the following areas:

1. A study can be conducted to evaluate the adult education programme of another centre of Baroda.
2. A study can be conducted on the effectiveness of existing monitoring system of the Adult Education Programme.
3. A study can be conducted on the impact of the Adult Education Programme on the adult learners.

4. The same study can be conducted with the following variables: a. Type of family, b. Marital status, c. Income of the family.
5. A study can be conducted on the role of income generating activities in motivating the adult learners in adult education centres of Baroda.
6. A study can be conducted on the extent of applying the knowledge gained in the adult education programme by the adult learners.

Appendices

Appendix-I

Profile of the Adult Learners

A: Background Infomration

The Following is the information regarding you and your family. Please read the following items carefully and tick mark (✓) your answers in the space provided below.

1) ____________________Name________________

2) ______________Address____________________

____

3) Age group you belong to:
   a) Below 20 years
   b) 21 – 25 years
   c) 26 – 30 years
   d) 31 – 35 years
   e) 36 – 40 years
   f) 46 – 50 years
   g) Above 50 years
4) Caste
   a) Schedule caste
   b) Schedule tribe
   c) General ___________
5) Religion
   a) Hindu___________

b) Muslim ______________
c) Christian ______________
d) Any other ______________

6) Type of house
   a) Kaccha house
   b) Puckka house
   c) Any other ______________

7) Type of the family
   a) Joint family
   b) Nuclear family

8) (i) Total number of family members (including yourself)
   ii) Number of
      a) Male members
      b) Female members

9) Occupation of the head of the family
   a) Business
   b) Service
   c) Labour
   d) Any other

10) Number of family members earning in your family
   a) One member
   b) Two members
   c) Three members
   d) Four members
   e) Or more

11) Total income of your family
   a) Rs. 1000–2000
   b) Rs. 2001–3000
   c) Rs. 3001–4000
   d) Rs. 4001–5000
   e) Rs. 5001–6000
   f) More than Rs. 6000

12) Your educational qualifications
   a) Primary
   b) Secondary
   c) Higher secondary
   d) Graduation
   e) Any other certificate course, diploma, etc.
13) Medium of instruction in your school / college
   a) Gujarati
   b) Hindi
   c) English
   d) If any other, please specify
14) Your marital status
   a) Unmarried
   b) Married
   c) Separated
   d) Widowed
15) (i) Are you employed?
   a) Yes
   b) No
16) Who encouraged you to be employed?
   a) Parents
   b) In-laws
   c) Husband
   d) Friends
   e) On your own
17) Your salary:
   a) Rs.500–1000
   b) Rs.1001–2000
   c) Rs.2001–3000
   d) Rs.3001– 4000
   e) More than Rs. 4000

18) Your work experience
    a) Less than one year
    b) 1-2 years
    c) 3-4 years
    d) More than four years
19) Your working hours
    a) 1-2 hours
    b) 3-4 hours
    c) 5-6 hours
    d) 7-8 hours
    e) More than 8 hours
20) Since how many years are you coming to 'Pragati Centre' to attend the Adult Education Programme?
    a) One year
    b) Two years
    c) Three years
    d) Four years
    e) More than four years
21) Number of adult education classes you have attended.
    a) 15 classes
    b) Less than 15 classes
22) Distance from your home to 'Pragati Centre'
    a) Less than 1 km
    b) 1-2 kms
    c) 3-4 kms
    d) 5-6 kms
    e) More than 6 kms
23) How do you come to the 'Pragati Centre'?
    a) On foot
    b) Bycycle
    c) By autorickshaw
    d) By bus

e) By your own vehicle

24) Who has encouraged you to join the adult education classes?

   a) Family members
   b) Local leader
   c) Relatives
   d) Friends
   e) Your own wish

25) i) Have you faced any opposition in the family to join the adult education classes?

   a) Yes
   b) No

   ii) If yes, from whom?

   a) Husband
   b) Family members
   c) Relatives
   d) If any other, please specify

B : Personality

Please read the following items carefully and encircle "T" if the item is applicable to you and "N" if the item is not applicable to you.

Sr.No.	*Statements*	*Yes*	*No*
1.	I enjoy social gatherings or parties.	Y	N
2.	My feelings change from happy to sad and sad to happy for no reason.	Y	N
3*.	I do not like to be leader at social functions.	Y	N
4.	I can do work even while people are looking on.	Y	N
5.	I like to change from one type of work to another very often.	Y	N
6*.	I become conscious of being observed in the presence of supervisors.	Y	N

(Contd...)

(Contd...)

7.	I am not afraid of being punished.	Y	N
8.	I like to have excitement (i.e., rousing to stimulation) in life.	Y	N
9.	My memory is good.	Y	N
10*.	I am unhappy most of the time.	Y	N
11*.	I worry over possible misfortune.	Y	N
12*.	I blush very often in the presence of others.	Y	N
13*.	I do not have a wide circle of friends.	Y	N
14.	One should act on suggestions quickly rather than stopping to think.	Y	N
15.	I do not like to keep quiet when out in a group.	Y	N
16.	Life is for getting pleasure.	Y	N
17.	I am not usually calm and collected most of the time.	Y	N
18.	I do not easily get tired of meeting people and talking to them.	Y	N
19*.	I would prefer to stay at home rather than attend a social function or party.	Y	N
20*.	I do not like public speaking.	Y	N

*Denotes negative statement

V.S. Shantamani and A. Hafeez's (1978) Personality scale and scoring pattern

Scoring Pattern	:	Y	N
Positive Statements	:	1	0
Negative Statements	:	0	1

0 – 10 scores indicates introvert personality

11 – 20 scores indicates extrovert personality

Frymier (1988) Junior index of motivation scale (JIM) and scoring pattern.

Score each item according to the following scale:.

+2 strongly agree

+1 agree

-1 disagree

-2 strongly disagree

Add each pupil's score algebraically. Then reverse the sign (if it is +18 change it to -18), (if it is -24 change it to +24) and then add this raw score value to 30 algebraically.

0 – 30 scores indicates low motivation

31 – 60 scores indicates high motivation.

C: Motivation

Please read each statement very carefully. There is no "right" or "wrong" answer. The best and only correct answer is your personal opinion. So, indicate your agreement and disagreement by marking it, according to the following scale, in. the appropriate space besides each statement. A - Strongly Agree, B - Agree, C - Disagree, & D - Strongly disagree

Sr. No. *Statements*	*Strongly Agree*	*Agree*	*Disagree*	*Strongly disagree*
1. Students should be made to go to school before they are 18 years old.	A	B	C	D
2. School is more fun when teachers let students do things they want to.	A	B	C	D
3. Pupils who try should get good grades even if they make mistakes.	A	B	C	D
4. Successful people are those who make the most money.	A	B	C	D
5. Most young people do not want to go to school.	A	B	C	D
6. The best people refuse to depend on other persons.	A	B	C	D
7. There are more important things in the world than making money.	A	B	C	D

(Contd...)

(Contd...)

8. Life is mostly sorrow with just a little joy.	A	B	C	D
9. Some students have to study more than others.	A	B	C	D
10. Being a good speaker is just as important as being a good speaker.	A	B	C	D
11. Some teachers seem to enjoy making students suffer.	A	B	C	D
12. Most people worry more before they a test than during the test.	A	B	C	D
13. Most people would like a school better if teachers did not give grades.	A	B	C	D
14. Most people just do not care for others.	A	B	C	D
15. Some people do not appreciate the value of education.	A	B	C	D

APPENDIX-II

OPINIONS OF ADULT LEARNERS

Curricular Aspect

The following is the list of statements regarding the curriculum of the Adult Education Programme of 'Pragati Centre'. Please give your opinions about it by encircling the appropriate choice.

GE - if you agree to a great extent, SE - if you agree to some extent, LE - If you agree to less extent.

Education

Sr. No	*Statements*	*Great Extent*	*Some Extent*	*Less Extent*
1.	Adult Education Programme provides the knowledge, which is useful in your day-to-day life.	GE	SE	LE
2.	Adult Education Programme helps in increasing the literacy level of the learners.	GE	SE	LE
3.	Adult Education Programme gives you different ideas of self-employment.GE	SE	LE	
4*.	Curriculum of the Adult Education Programme is not useful because women indulge only in gossiping.	GE	SE	LE
5*.	The content taught in the class is of no use as no further guidance is given to what should be done afterwards.	GE	SE	LE
6*.	The content taught in the Adult Education Programme have too many ideas, which confuse you.	GE	SE	LE
7*.	The content taught in the Adult Education Programme is difficult to understand.	GE	SE	LE

(Contd...)

(Contd...)

8.	The content taught is remembered even after the completion of the class.	GE	SE	LE
9.	The Adult Education Programme teaches you many things besides the content—discipline, handling different situations, etc.	GE	SE	LE
10.	The Adult Education Programme fulfills the purpose with which you joined the programme.	GE	SE	LE

B: Self-developemnt

Sr. No	*Statements*	*Great Extent*	*Some Extent*	*Less Extent*
1	You have started taking decisions in the family matters.	GE	SE	LE
2.	You have started putting your decisions into action.	GE	SE	LE
3.	You have developed the feeling of independence.	GE	SE	LE
4.	You have become open in sharing your ideas with others.	GE	SE	LE
5.	You have developed a sense of accomplishment.	GE	SE	LE
6.	You have started discussing and solving the problems of your community.	GE	SE	LE
7.	You have become strong to express yourself if you are subjected to any form of injustice.	GE	SE	LE
8.	You have developed the ability of communicating with different people.	GE	SE	LE
9.	You have become confident in interacting with others.	GE	SE	LE
10.	You have developed a feeling of having an ambition in your life.	GE	SE	LE

C: Health

Sr. No	Statements	Great Extent	Some Extent	Less Extent
1.	You have become concerned about your diet.	GE	SE	LE
2.	You have become concerned about health of your family members.	GE	SE	LE
3.	You have become concerned about the nutritious diet of your family members.	GE	SE	LE
4.	You have started cooking new recipes keeping in mind its nutritive value.	GE	SE	LE
5.	You have become curious to find new recipes.	GE	SE	LE

D: Creativity

Sr. No	Statements	Great Extent	Some Extent	Less Extent
1.	You have started making creative articles such as lampshade, artificial flowers, etc.	GE	SE	LE
2.	You have decorated your home with different creative articles or showpieces.	GE	SE	LE
3.	You have started thinking that you can generate income by making creative articles.	GE	SE	LE
4.	You have created beautiful articles out of waste materials.	GE	SE	LE
5.	You have started collecting innovative ideas for making creative articles.	GE	SE	LE

E: Instructor Aspect

The following is the list of statements regarding the instructors who taught you in the Adult Education Programme in 'Pragati Centre'. Please give your opinions about the instructors by encircling your choice.

GE - if you agree to a great extent, SE- if you agree to some extent, LE - if you agree to less extent.

Sr. No	*Statements*	*Great Extent*	*Some Extent*	*Less Extent*
1.	They were sympathetic.	GE	SE	LE
2.	They were helping and caring.	GE	SE	LE
3.	They were impartial with the learners.	GE	SE	LE
4.	They were friendly.	GE	SE	LE
5.	They were able to maintain the discipline in the adult education classes.	GE	SE	LE
6.	They taught in an interesting manner.	GE	SE	LE
7.	They were punctual in the Adult Education Classes.	GE	SE	LE
8.	They gave solutions to your queries.	GE	SE	LE
9.	The language was clearly understood.	GE	SE	LE
10.	Their voice was clear and loud.	GE	SE	LE
11.	They taught according to the pace of learning.	GE	SE	LE
12.	They gave equal opportunities to all to participate in the adult education programme.	GE	SE	LE
13.	They enthusiastically discussed their ideas and experiences, e.g. regarding AIDS, reproductive system etc.	GE	SE	LE
14.	They were confident while conducting the Adult Education Programme.	GE	SE	LE
15.	They described the same thing in different ways to give a clear understanding.	GE	SE	LE

F: Physical Aspects

The following is the list of statement regarding the physical condition of 'Pragati Centre', Please give your opinions by encircling: GE - if you agree to a great extent, SE - if you agree to some extent, LE- if you agree to a less extent.

Sr. No	*Statements*	*Great Extent*	*Some Extent*	*Less Extent*
1.	It was convenient for you to have a full view of demonstration.	GE	SE	LE
2.	There was adequate light to see clearly.	GE	SE	LE
3.	There was proper ventilation.	GE	SE	LE
4.	There was comfortable sitting arrangement.GE	SE	LE	
5.	The timing of the classes was convenient to you.	GE	SE	LE

G: Methods and Materials Aspect

The following is a checklist regarding the methods and materials. Please give your opinions regarding the same by a tick mark in the space provided below:

GE - if you like to a great extent, SE - if you like to some extent LE - if you like to a less extent

1) Teaching aids were used by the instructors in the programme.

   a) Yes ___________

   b) No ___________

2) Teaching aids were well prepared.

   a) Yes ___________

   b) No ___________

3) To what extent you found the following teaching methods effective?

a) Demonstration	GE	SE	LE
b) Workshop	GE	SE	LE
c) Discussion	GE	SE	LE
d) Drama	GE	SE	LE
e) Educational talk	GE	SE	LE

4) To what extent you found the following teaching aids effective?

a) Posters	GE	SE	LE
b) Flashcards	GE	SE	LE
c) Flipcharts	GE	SE	LE
d) Models	GE	SE	LE
e) Specimens	GE	SE	LE
f) Photographs	GE	SE	LE

5) Mention the name of recipes you prepared at home, after having learnt it through demonstration________________.

6) Mention the name of articles you prepared at home, after having learnt it through demonstration________________.

ANNEXURE III

REASONS FOR NOT ATTENDING

The following is a list of statements regarding the reasons for not attending the Adult Education classes in 'Pragati Centre' of the Department of Home Science Extension and Communication. Please encircle: Y - if the item is applicable to you, N - if the item is not applicable to you

Sr.No	*Reasons*	*Yes*	*No*
1.	You did not know the exact time of the class.	Y	N
2.	You did not know the place where the classes were conducted.	Y	N
3.	You were not informed about the activities of the adult education classes.	Y	N
4.	The timings of the adult education classes were not convenient for you.	Y	N
5.	You were tired because of household work.	Y	N
6.	You had to look after a young child in the family.	Y	N
7.	You had to look after one of your family members who was sick at home.	Y	N
8.	You were sick when adult education classes were going on.	Y	N
9.	You thought that you do not have much creativity as others have.Y	N	
10.	It was expensive for you to come to 'Pragati Centre' because of the long distance from home to 'Pragati Centre'.	Y	N
11.	You had to go for your part-time/full-time job at the same time as the adult education classes.	Y	N
12.	It was the time for your husband to come home from office.	Y	N
13.	It was the time for your children to return home from school.	Y	N

(Contd...)

(Contd...)

14.	You thought that it was not worth attending the classes, as you were not going to get any job after attending the adult education classes.	Y	N
15.	You had to go to other classes at the same time, like beauty parlour, stitching classes, etc.	Y	N

Appendix IV

Suggestions by the Adult Learner

The following is a list of suggestions for the Adult Education Programme of 'Pragati Centre'. Please give your suggestions in the space provided by encircling your choice.

GE - If you agree to a great extent, SE - If you agree to some extent, LE - If you agree to less extent.

Sr. No	*Statements*	*Great Extent*	*Some Extent*	*Less Extent*
1.	Awareness regarding marketing strategies should be provided to sell the products.	GE	SE	LE
2.	Further guidance to what should be done afterwards can make the programme more meaningful.	GE	SE	LE
3.	More opportunities should be provided for self-expression.	GE	SE	LE
4.	A childcare centre facility should be provided so that women can attend the Adult Education Programme free from the worry of their children.	GE	SE	LE
5.	Computer education should be provided.GE	SE	LE	
6.	Adequate transport arrangement should be made	GE	SE	LE

(Contd...)

(Contd...)

7.	Exhibition can be put up for the products made in the adult education classes.	GE	SE	LE
8.	A library facility should be provided which would develop reading habits and increase knowledge.	GE	SE	LE
9.	Aspect of the programme you think needs renewal. a) Instructors training b) Management of the programme	GE GE	SE SE	LE LE

10. Please give your suggestions for the effectiveness and the success of the Adult Education Programme.

____

____

____

____

Suggestions by the UBS/UCD Community Volunteers and Teacher Supervisors

The following is the list of suggestions for the Adult Education Programme of 'Pragati Centre'. Please give your suggestions in the space provided by encircling your choice:

GE - If you agree to great extent, SE - If you agree to some extent, LE- If you agree to less extent.

Sr. No	*Statements*	*Great Extent*	*Some Extent*	*Less Extent*
1.	Thoughtful attention should be given to the needs of the learners.	GE	SE	LE
2.	There should be an openness, which eases the expression of views on the part of the adult learners.	GE	SE	LE

(Contd...)

(Contd...)

3.	Awareness regarding marketing strategies should be provided to sell the products.	GE	SE	LE
4.	Computer education should be provided.GE	SE	LE	
5.	Adequate transport arrangement should be made.	GE	SE	LE
6.	A library facility should be provided which would develop reading habits and increase knowledge.	GE	SE	LE
7.	A childcare centre facility should be provided so that women can attend the adult education programme free from the worry of their children.	GE	SE	LE
8.	Professional guidance should be given to the adult learners.	GE	SE	LE
9.	Aspects of the programme you think need renewal			
	a) Management of the programme	GE	SE	LE
	b) Instructors training	GE	SE	LE

10. Please give your suggestions for the effectiveness and success of the adult education programme:

____

____

____

____

Bibliography

ADISESHIAH, M. S. Adult education and development (the Dar-es-salam conference). *Indian Journal of Adult Education*. 1977.

ALEEM S. *Women's Development Problems and Prospects*. APH Publishing Corporation, 5, Ansari Road, Darya Ganj, New Delhi,1996.

ANANTHANARAYANA H.S. Evaluation of adult literacy material in Kannada, *Indian Journal of Adult Education*, Vol.40. No.3, March 1979.

ANSARI. N.A. *Adult Education in India*. S. Chand & Co. New Delhi, 1984.

ARYAN, C.S. A study of Gravin County homemakers and why members drop out of home demonstration clubs. *Review of Extension Research*. Circular 541: 43- 44. September 1962.

ATHREYA. V.B. Chunkath S. Literacy and Empowerment, Sage Publications India Pvt Ltd., New Delhi, 1996

ATIENZA, MARIA FE G. Extra-Mural education for women. *The Indian Journal of Adult Education*. 34 (2), Feb. 1973.

AXFORD, ROGER W. Adult Educaiton, *The Open Door, Coordinator of Adult Education University of Naine*. International textbook Co. Scramton, Pennsylvania, 1994.

BARGE, U. B. A study of people's participation in the programme conducted by the Labour Welfare Centre, Baroda. Unpublished M.S.W. Thesis, M.S.University of Baroda, 1962.

BARTHAKUR, D. Problems faced by the Mukhya Sevikas in Implementing the Applied Nutrition Programme in Gujarat. Unpublished Thesis (M.Sc.) M.S. University, Baroda, 1980.

BASTIA K.C. Adult education for tribals in Orissa - some problems, *Indian Journal of Adult Education*, Vol.42. No.4, April 1981.

BHANDARI, J. Factors Affecting Persistency and Dropout of Adult literacy Classes in Udaipur District. (Ph.D.) Agri. Udai. U., 1974,

Abstract No. 789, p. 54. In Buch, M.B., ed. Survey of Research in Education.

BHATIA, NISHI, KUMAR G.A.K. A study on neo-literates of Delhi Sarv Shiksha Abhiyan, *Indian Journal of Adult Education,* Vol.62. No.1, January-March 2001.

BHATNAGAR, S. Nutrition education through traditional aids. *The Indian Journal of Home Science.* 14 (4), 1982,

BHATTY, I.Z. Inequality and Poverty in Rural India. In *Poverty and Income Distribution in India.* Calcutta, Statistical Publishing Society, 1976.

BHOLA , H.S., Description and evaluation of training program for literacy teachers and their trainers, *Indian Journal of Adult Education,* Vol. XXXI. No.5, May 1970.

BISHNOI, INDIRA, Reasons given by the women for not attending the adult education classes conducted by the labour welfare centre, Dissertation (M. Sc), M.S. University, Baroda, 1978.

BRAR, SURINDAR K. Job satisfaction of collage home science teachers of Punjab, M.Sc. Thesis, Faculty of Home Science M.S. University, Baroda, 1984.

BRYAN. C.S. A study of Gravin country home makers and why members dropout of home demonstration clubs. *Review of Extension Research.* Circular 541:43-44 September 1962.

BWATAVA, Y. A Descriptive Study of a Programme charged with Reduction of Illiteracy in Tanzania. Ball State University, Thesis, (Ed.D), A dissertation Abstracts International, 1976.

CHANDRA S.K, Fifty years of Indian Administration -Retrospect's and prospects: women and empowerment, *The Indian Journal of public administration.* Volume: XLIII No-3, July-Sept. 1997.

CHANDRA, A. Adult education in home making. *Indian Journal of Adult Education.* 1973, 17 (B), 11.

CHANDRA, A.R. and SAXENA, *T.P. Style Manual for Writing Theses, Dissertations and Papers in Social Sciences.* New Delhi, Metropolitan Book Co., 1979.

CHARLES A. ISBEN and Manuel Alers-Mantalro. Expressed family needs, in L.S. Saraswathi's process for identifying educational needs of adults. Unpublished Doctoral's thesis, Iowa State University, Ames, Iowa, 1969.

CHETANLAL NEERA, Relative effectivness of graphic aids and projected aids enriched with museum experiences, in teaching food and digestion to VIII standard students of Navrachna Higher Secondary School, Baroda 1983. Dissertation (M.Sc.)- Faculty of Home Science, M.S. University, Baroda, 1983.

CHICKERMANE, D.V. An experiment in continuation education for school leavers after the compulsory education age limit of elelven, Gargoti 1966. (Abstract in, Buch M.B., ed. *A Survey of Reserach in Education,* CASE, M. S. University of Baroda, 1974).

CHOMCHEUM Thongpleu, A study of non-formal Vocational education programme in the educational region of Thailand, Dissertation (Ph.D), CASE, M.S. University, Baroda, 1984.

CHOMSRI WICHAI, A study of non-formal education in Thailand, Dissertation (M.Ed.), CASE, M.S. University, Baroda, 1989.

CHUG SUN, N. M. The orientation towards non participation in adult education. *A Dissertation Abstracts International,* 1976, 36 (1), 4199A.

COOMBS, PHILIP, New paths of Learning, *Teacher today,* April-June 1976. Directorate of Primary and Secondary education, Rajasthan, Bikaner, India.

DAMODARAN, M. The child health card. *Nutrition,* 8 (1), 26, 1974,

DANGI K.L., S.R. MEENA, BANSAL VISHAKHA, Factors motivating adults in total literacy campaign, *Indian Journal of Adult Education,* Vol.63. No.3, July-September 2002.

DAS P.K., KALITA D.C., SHARMA T.K., Impact of literacy campaign on health, hygiene, conservation of Environment and national integration in Pragjyotishpur of Assam, *Indian Journal of Adult* Education, Vol.63. No.3, July-September 2002.

DESSE. JAMES. *Psychology of Learning*. McGraw Book Co. Inc., New York, Toronto, London, 1952.

DEVADAS, R. Whither the National Adult Education. *Indian J. Adult Education.* 1979, 40(10).

DHAMA, O.P. and BHATNAGAR, O.P. *Education and Communication for Development*. New Delhi. Oxford and IBH Publishing Co., 1980.

DUTTA S.C., *Adult Education in Third World,* Criterion Publishers. New Delhi, 1987.

Education in India (1984- 85), Report, Ministry of Education and youth Services, Government of India, Vol. 1, 1970,

EDWARDS, A.L. *Techniques of Attitude Scale Construction.* Bombay, Vakils, Feffer and Simons Pvt. Ltd., 1969.

GARRET, H.E. *Statistics in Psychology and Education*. New Delhi, Longmans Green & Co., 1973.

GAYATONDE. Problems of Social Education in India with special Reference to the States of Maharashtra, Gujarat, Rajasthan, Madhya Pradesh and Mysore. (Ph.D.) Edu., Poona U., Abstract No. 794, p. 543. In Buch, M.B., ed. *Survey of Research in Education,* 1977,

General education and technical education and developmental research, National planning Committees series reports of sub-committees.: Vora and Company, Bombay, 1948.

GHOSH SUBUMAN, SIKDAR DEB PRASAD, Impact of Mass literacy programme among the children (9-14 years) of tribal belt of Sundaban Area, *Indian Journal of Adult Education,* Vol.61. No.4, October - December 2000.

GIREESAN K., Role of local government institutions in the implementation of continuing education programme in Kerala, *Indian Journal of Adult Education,* Vol.61. No.3, July-September 2000.

GIRI, V.V. Adult Education for women in the changing society. *Indian Journal of Adult Education,* 33 (12) Dec. 1974.

GOYAL RUCHI, An action project to institute a short term Non Formal Education course in the Department of Home Science Extension and Communication for adolescent girls and women for income generation and self-development, Dissertation (M. Sc), M.S. University, Baroda, 1996.

GROVER R.R., CHOPRA RITA, *Adult Education,* The Indian Publication, Ambala Cantt, 1998.

GUPTA SANDHYA, A comparative study of three visual aids in imparting non-formal education to urban adolescent girls and young women belonging to the three labour welfare centre, Dissertation (M. Sc), M.S. University, Baroda, 1986.

GUPTA, A. A study of differences in leisure time interests of home makers of three selected sub-urban colonies of Baroda. Unpublished M.Sc.(Home) thesis, M.S. University of Baroda, 1974.

HAZARIKA SULTANA, Reasons given by the adult women for not attending the adult education classes in Home Science with respect to their SES and age, Dissertation (M. Sc), M.S. University, Baroda, 1971.

HESTER CHADDERDON and MARY S, LYLE, *Reasons given by Iova Woman for Attending Home Making Glasses for Adults,* Iowa State Collage, Amos, Iowa, 1955.

HIRANYAMALINI S., A study of worries of adult of Kamatipura, Baroda, Dissertation (M. Sc), M.S. University, Baroda, 1972.

HOUL, C. O. *Continuing Your Education.* London : McGraw Hill Book Company, 1964.

India, An Outline : Directorate of Non-formal (Adult) Education, Ministry of Education and Social Welfare, New Delhi, 1978.

INDIA, EDUCATION COMMISSION. *Report of the Education Commission (1964-66)*. Ministry of Education, New Delhi, 1966.

India, *Non-formal Education* (Preparatory work for the implementation of the scheme for 15-35 age group), Directorate of Non-formal (Adult) education, Ministry of Education and Social Welfare, New Delhi, Nov. 1975.

India, *Non-formal Education in the Fifth Five Year Plan*, Directorate of Non-formal Education, Ministry of Education and Social Welfare, New Delhi, 1974.

Innovative Approaches to Functional Literacy for poverty Alleviation, National Case Study India; UNESCO & Indian National Commission, for co-operation with UNESCO, Ministry of Human Resource Development, New Delhi, 2000.

IOVAL SPAFFORD AND EDNA P. AMIDON. *Studies of home economics in high school and adult education programme*, 1955-1958 Washington D.C. U.S.Govt. 1968.

IYER V. MEENA, A study of classroom climate and pupil academic motivation in two schools of Baroda city, Dissertation (M. Ed.), CASE, M.S. University, Baroda, 1988.

JANI M, *Empowerment of women: A study of level of self esteem, decision making and family support among women of Baroda city*, 1999.

JANSEN GALE, LIVERRIGHT, A.A AND HELLENBECK WILBUR. *Adult Education*. Association of the U.S.A, U.S.A. 1964.

JAYAWEERA, S. Programme of nonformal education for women. Indian Journal of Adult Education. 40(12) Dec. 1979.

JHANSI SC, MISHRA K. Santosh, Urban adult education -issues for concern, *Indian Journal of Adult Education*, Vol.61. No. 4, October-December 2000.

KAMALADEVI Spiritual and Moral Education, *Education of Women in Modern India*, Aundh Published Trust, Aundh, 1946

KANITKAR, H. Puppets for consientisation: Few Cases. *Interaction* 1(3), 1933.

KAUR, BAL PARAMIOVDER. Problems of the teacher and organiser in conducting and organising adult education programme in selected subject matter areas for the women form the weaker sections of Baroda. M.Sc. thesis, Faculty of Home science, M.S. University, Baroda, 1981,

KEMPFER, HOMER AND HELEN. *Selected Problems in Social Education*. Indian Adult Education Association. 17- B, Indraprastha marg, New Delhi, 1963.

KHURANA, KANWAL. Reasons Given by the Adult Women of selected Communities of Baroda for attending Adult Education

Classes conducted by the Home Science Education and Extension Department of the Faculty of Home Science, Baroda, unpublished M.Sc. (Home) Thesis, Baroda, M.S. University of Baroda, 1970.

KJELBERG, SHIRLEY. A Study of knowledge gained by women enrolled in the adult home- making programs in Iowa schools. *Abstract of Masters Thesis,* Mankato State College, 1968. Interstate Library Loan. Home Economics Research Abstracts 1969.

KLEIN PAUL E. AND RUTH E. MOFITT. *Counseling techniques in adult education.* McGraw Hill Book Co, Inc., London, N.Y. 1938

KUMAR RAJESH, SINGH KULVINDER, SINGH HARBANS, Literacy and educability in rural community in Himachal Pradesh: A case study, *Indian Journal of Adult Education,* Vol.61. No.4, October-December 2000.

KUPPUSWAMY, B. *Mannual of Socio-economic Status Scale* (Urban). Delhi: Mansayan, 1962.

KWEKA A.N., Adult education for self-reliance in community health education programme - A case study from Tanzania, *Adult Education and Development,* No.42, 1994.

LEAGANS, J. P. *Characteristics of teaching and learning in extension education.* In *Extension education in community development.* New Delhi: Directorate of Extension, Ministry of Foods and Agriculture, Government of India, 1961.

Literacy for Empowerment. National Literacy Mission, Ministry of Human Resource Development, Government of India, 2000.

MADLER, L. Business and industry. In Smith, A. & Kidd. *Handbook of adult education.* U.S.A. Publication of Adult education association, 1970.

MATHUR M. BRIJENDRA, *Adult education and social change,* The Indian Publication, Ambala Cantt, 1989.

MATHUR R.S., Training Program for adult education personnel -their evaluation, *Indian Journal of Adult Education,* Vol.42. No.3, March 1981.

MATHUR V.S., *Handbook for adult education instructors,* Indian Adult Education Association Delhi, 1980.

MELLON, D. A comparison of characteristics and factors of adult education participants enrolled in two selected schools in oplahanacity. A Dissertation Abstracts International, 1975, 35 (8), 4163A

MINISTRY OF EDUCATION AND YOUTH SERVICES, Government of India. *Education in India,* Vol. 1, 1970.

MISHRA S.N. *Poverty and its Alleviation.* Deep & Deep Publication PVT.LTD. New Delhi. 2005.

MISTRY S.P.; *Non-Formal Education: An approach to education for all.* Radha Publications, New Delhi. 1998.

MITRA. J. *Women and Society: Equality and Empowerment,* Kanishka publication, New Delhi, 1997.

MOHANTY, JAGANNATH, *Adult and Non-formal Education,* Deep publication New Delhi, 1991.

MOHSINI S.R., J.L. SACHDEV, ASHA SEHGAL, *Towards a Comprehensive Adult Education Program,* Indian Adult Education Association, New Delhi, 2002.

MOODY, L. R. The effectiveness of contacting non attending adult students as measured by return attendance dropouts and reenrollment. *A Dissertation Abstracts International.* 1977, 37 (9), 5531A.

MULLIKAYNASWAMY, M. Survey of Reading Needs and Interests of Adult Neo-literates in Mysore State, Mysore State Adult Education Council, Mysore. Abstract No. 800, p. 545. In Buch, M.B.ed. *Survey of Research in Education,* 1969.

MUNN, O.H. An analysis of characteristics and attitudes of participants in short term continuing education classes in an urban situation. *A Dissertation Abstracts. International,* 1975, 37 (11), 7013A

NADLER, L. Business and Industry. In Smith A. & Kidd. *Handbook of Adult Education.* U,S.A. Publication of Adult Education Association, 1970.

NAGAPPA, T.R. Survey of Reading Needs and Interests of Adult Neo-literates in Mysore State, Mysore State Adult Education Council. NCERT, Abstract No. 686, p. 536. In Buch, M.B. ed., *Survey of Research in Education.*

NATARAJAN, V. *Evaluation report on the performance of adult literacy programme in Bihar.* Directorate of Adult Education, Bihar, Patna, 1981.

NATH, SHAM, *Report on International Conference on Adult Education.* Indian Adult Education Association. 17-B, Indraprastha Marg, New Delhi, 1961.

NIMBALKAR M.R. *Adult education.* Mittal publication, Delhi, 1987.

OMORUYI F.E.O, The dilemma of women in adult literacy education programme in Benin Metropolis, *Indian Journal of Adult Education,* Vol.62. No.1, January-March 2001, 55-68.

OPPENHEIM, A.N. *Questionnaire Design and Attitude Measurement.* London, Heinemann Education Books Ltd., 1970.

ORME, N. An analysis of characteristics, and attitudes of participants in short-term Contuinuing Education Classes in an urban situation. A Dissertation Abstracts International. A Humanities and Soc. Sci., 37(11) No. 1976 : 7013-A.

OTTEN, MABEL, Adult education follows social needs. *Journal of Homeeconomics*, Vol. 49, p.137, May 1957.

PANDEY V.C, *Literacy and Non-Formal Education* (2005), Isha Books Publication, Adarsh Nagar, Delhi

PARLIKAR, K.R. Relationship of certain factors to the interest and participation of the members from three selected Mahila mandals of Bulsar district, Baroda. Unpublished M.Sc. (Home) thesis, M. S. University of Baroda, 1966.

PATEL MALINI, Attitude of women towards the selected areas of non-formal education program for women from the weaker section of Baroda, Dissertation (M. Sc.), M.S. University, Baroda, 1981.

PATEL V, *Women's Challenges of the New Millennium*, Gyan Publishing House, New Delhi, 2002.

PATEL, G. An investigation to study the Attitudes of the Teacher Educators towards the Programmes of Non-formal Education leading to life long Education in the State of Gujarat. Unpublished Thesis (Ph.D.), M. S. University of Baroda, 1979.

PATEL, R.B. A Critical Study of Social Education in the State of Gujarat, Ph.D. Edu., SPU, 1970. Abstract No. 689, p. 538. In Buch, M.B. ed. *Survey of Research in Education.*

PATEL, S. A study of Activities of three Labour welfare Centres in Baroda City and Women Participation. Unpublished Thesis (M.S.W.). M. S. University, Baroda 1978.

PATHAK, MANISHA, Effectiveness of Puppetary as a method for educating rural adult women. Dissertation (M.Sc.) - Faculty of Home Science, The M.S. University, Baroda, 1984.

PERDIUE MARY JANE. Reasons for participation of select groups of low income women in 'sewing classes' Master's Southern Illinois University, 1967. Interlibrary Loan, *Home Economics Research Abstract*. 1967.

PILLAI SIVADASAN K., Adult / non-formal education programme in India Legislative, conceptual and evaluative analysis, *Indian Journal of Adult Education*, Vol. 41. No. 5, May 1990.

POLLARD, L. BELLE. *Adult Education for home making, supervisor Household*. Arts Public Schools. Saint Louis, Missouri, 2002.

PRASHANT, GANGULI K. PATHAK K.N., MIRZA SHANAZ, Adult education in Bihar: An appraisal, *Indian Journal of Adult Education*, Vol. 46. No. 2, February 1985.

RAI A., *Distance Education Open Learning Vs Virtual University Concepts* (2000), India at Tarun Offset publication, Delhi, 2000.

RAJU, SURAPA S. AKSHARA SANKRANTHI Programme: An evaluation, *Indian Journal of Adult Education*, Vol.63. No.4, October-December 2002.

RANI SUDHA, ESWARAIAH G., Study on mass media exposure of neo-literates in continuing education centers, *Indian Journal of Adult Education,* Vol.63. No.3, July-September 2002.

RAO, B. The case for Non- formal education. Indian Journal of Adult Education, 36(5), 1973:

RASHID. ABDUR. Experimental adult schools. Research Training and Production Centre, The Jamia Millia. ARTP Publication No.30, New Delhi.

RASTOGI K.G., Evaluation of national adult education program, *Indlun Journal of Adult Education,* Vol.39. No. 11-12, November-December 1978.

RATHORE BINDU, An action project on imparting training in puppetry to UBS/UCD Community Volunteers of Baroda Municipal Corporation, Dissertation (M. Sc), M.S. University, Baroda, 1997.

RAUCH, DAVID B. *Priorities in Adult Education,* A publication of the Adult Education Association of the USA, 1998.

REDDY G. Lokanadha, Personality characteristics affecting participation in adult education program: A study, *Indian Journal of Adult Education,* Vol.47. No.8, August 1986.

REDDY P. ADINARAYANA, Evaluation of training program of Non-formal education functionaries, *Indian Journal of Adult Education,* Vol.46. No. 12, December 1985.

ROY RANJAN NIKHIL, *Adult education in India and Abroad,* S.Chand & Co. New Delhi, 1967.

RUANGURAI SRINILTA. Reasons for participation in women and youth group in two development areas of Thailand. Master's, Lowa State University 1967. Interlibrary Loan Home Economics Research Abstracts 1967.

SANGHMITRA SAIKIA, A study of institutional climate of selected institute offering higher education in Home Science in Gujarat, Dissertation (M.Sc), M.S.University, Baroda, 1986

SATYANARAYANA, P., SESHARATNAM, C. *Distance Education. What? Why? How?,* Booklinks Corporation, Hyderabad,2000.

SAXENA RADHA RANI, Changing roles of Indian women in society, Social Welfare, Vol.48. No.5, August 2001.

SHAH and WRIGHT. *Scales for the Measurement of Attitudes.* New York, McGraw, 1967.

SHAH K.R., *Adult Education Programme in Gujarat third Evaluation,* Sardar Patel Institute of Economic and Social Research, Ahemdabad, 1983.

SHAH, ANUPAMA. A Critical Study of the Programmes of Non-formal Education in Baroda City and their Impact on the Community. Unpublished Thesis (Ph.D.), M.S.University, Baroda, 1978.

SHAH, G. B. Non formal education for Women. *Indian Journal of Adult Education,* 33 (11), 1977.

____________ Non formal education for women. Indian Journal of Adult Education, 1977, 38 (11), 14.

SHARMA ANURADHA, Comparative study of attitudes of rural and urban adult learners towards literacy campaign, *Indian Journal of Adult Education,* Vol.61. No.4, October-December 2000.

SHARMA ATUL, SHAH P. VIMAL, PARIKH K BHANUMATI, *Adult Education Programme in Gujarat*: An appraisal, Sardar Patel Institute of Economic and Social Research, Ahemdabad, 1979.

____________ SHARAN G., D.R. VEENA, PARIKH K. BHANUMATI, Adult education in India, Anmol publication New Delhi, 1989.

SHARMA INDER, PATEL SUSHIL, Adult education programme in Chandigarh:an empirical study, *Indian Journal of Adult Education.* Vol.47. No.5, May 1986.

SHARMA NEERJA, KHANDAI HEMANTA, Moving continuing education towards learning society, *Indian Journal of Adult Education,* Vol.62. NO.4, October December 2001.

SHARMA S.R.; *Reflections on Continuing and Non formal Education;* Pointer Publisher, Jaipur; 1997.

SHARMA, D.U. & SHARMA, K.D. Working of instructors in adult education centers of IAEA, *Indian Journal of Adult Education,* 42 (5), 1981.

SHARMA, K.D. *The Role of Women in India.* Peace Education, 1971, 1 (1).

SHARMA, S. *Distance Education.* Omsons Publications, New Delhi, 1999.

SHARMA, T.R. Adult education in Punjab : An investigation, *Indian Journal of Adult Education.* Vol. XXXII, No. 2, 1971,

SHEAS, PAUL H. CLARENCE D. JAYNA AND RALPH D. SPENCE. Ways means and methods in adult education. *Adult education,* New York, The Dryden Press, 1953.

SHIRUR, RAJANI R. *Non-formal Education for Development;* APH Publishing Corporation, New Delhi; 1995.

SHUKLA MAMTA, The effectiveness of communication through demonstration and workshop in NFE centre - Pragati. Department of Home Science Extension and Communication, Dissertation (M. Sc), M.S. University, Baroda, 1985.

SINGH B. *New Horizons in Distance Education.* B.S. Uppal for Uppal publications, New Delhi, 1995.

SINGH J.L., K.D. GAUR; *Need for New Strategies to Eradicate Poverty;* Manak publications PVT. LTD, New Delhi; 1999.

SINGH MADAN, *Adult Education in 21st Century,* The Associated Publishers, Ambala Cantt, 2001.

SINGH RANJIT, Life-long education: Present status and future strategy, *Indian Journal of Adult Education,* Vol.62. No.4, October-December 2001.

SINGH, R.O. The Communication Ideas through adult education in India, 1957. Abstracted in, Buch, M.S. University, Baroda, 1974.

SINGH, R.P. Audiovisual aids in adult education. *Indian Journal of Adult Education.* 32 (11) New. 1971.

SINGH, SOHAN. *History of Adult Education During British Period.* Indian Adult Education Association. Delhi, 1957.

SINGH, U., SUDARSHAN, K. *Distance Education.* Discovery Publishing House, New Delhi, 2000.

SINHA ANIL, K. *Adult Education and Social Change.* Directorate of Adult Education, Bihar, Patna, 1979.

SOUNDARAPANDIAN, M. *Literacy Campaign in India* (2000), Discovery Publishing House, New Delhi

SRIVASTAVA, L. R. N Identification of educational problems of the Saore of Orrisa, Tribal Education Unit, N C E R T, New Delhi, 1970. Abstracted in, Buch, M.S. ed. *A Survey of Research in Education,* CASE, The M.S. University, Baroda, 1974,

TAKHAR HARJIT KAUR, Educational aspirations of drop-outs among rural adolescent girls and factors responsible for dropping out of school, Dissertation (M. Sc), M.S. University, Baroda, 1986.

TALUKDAR, B.K. Adult Education in Assam during Past Independence Period. Gau. Univ., 1975, Thesis (Ph.D.), Abstract No. 805. p. 547. *Second Survey of Research in Education* (ed. by Buch, M.B.), 1979.

THAKUR ANITA, Problems and job satisfaction of adult literacy teachers of Dabhoi Taluka of Baroda district, ...Dissertation (M. Sc), M.S. University, Baroda, 1986.

TRIVEDI, R.S. A Critical study of social Education programmes and procedures in Katra district. 1966. Abstracted in such, M.B. Ed. A *Survey of research in education,* CASE, The M.S. University, Baroda, 1974.

UNESCO. *Report on Community Development Programmes,* Kurukshetra, 6(2), Oct. 1961

VANOVER, J. A Survey of the attitude of Adult Basic Education Students in Mississippi. Dissertation Abstract International: A. Humanities and Soc. Sci., 40(3), Sept., 1979: 1210-A.

VENKATAIAH S.; *Non-formal Education*. Anmol Publications Pvt. LTD, New Delhi. 2004.

VENKATAIAH, N. Impact of the Farmer's functional literacy Programme on the Participants in Andhra Pradesh, Ph.D. Edu., SVU. Abstract No. 306, p. 548. In Buch, M.B.Ed., *Survey of Research in Education*, 1977.

VENKATAPPA R. and REDDY M.M., National demonstration scheme in Chittor district: An appraisal, *Indian Journal of Adult Education*, Vol.44. No.4, April 1982.

VIJAYARAGHAWAN, K. Ecological constraints and nutrition status of the community. *Nutrition*. 1974, 8 (3).

VYAS V.S., Pradeep Bhargava; *Poverty Reduction in Developing Countries Experiences from Asia & Africa*; Rawat Publications. Jaipur and New Delhi; 1999.

WIESINGER, RITA. Economic development and functional Literacy for Women. *Internation Review of Education*. XIX/1073/1.

WRUGHSTONE, J. *Evaluation in Modern Education*. New York: American Book Company, 1956.

YADAV SINGH RAJENDRA, *Adult Education Training and Productivity*, The Indian Publication, Ambala Cantt, 1991.

YOUSEFF. H. NADIA, SADKA NANCY, MARPHY ERNEST, *An evaluation of non-formal education programmes for women* in Morocco, Women in Development Agency for International Development, New State Washington, 1992.

WEBLIOGRAPHY

http://www.chandigarhtrafficpolice.org/safety_tips_kids_pedestrian/Kids_school_area_safety_section.php

http://auto.indiamart.com/user-manual/road-regulation.html

http://www.nlm.nic.in/women.htm

http ://www.tradechakra. com/indian-economy/poverty-in-india.html

http://www.surfindia.com/automobile/traffic-rules.html

http ://en. wikipedia. org/wiki/Traffic_sign

http://www.education.nic.in/cd50years/y/3T/9Q/3T9Q0301.htm

http://www.infed.org/biblio/b-nonfor.htm

http://www.indianetzone.com/39/non_formal education india.htm

http://socserv.mcmaster.ca/soc/courses/stpp4C03/ClassEssay/literacy.htm

http://www.ed.gov

http://www.nsba.org/sbot/toolkit/teie.html

http://www.unicef.org/infobycountry/india_statistics.html

www.nlm.nic.in/tlc_nlm.htm

www.ask.com

www.google.com

Index